Common Good

Common Good

Ideas from the Humphrey

Edited by

John E. Brandl

Hubert H. Humphrey Institute of Public Affairs
Minneapolis
2006

On the cover

The logo of the Hubert H. Humphrey Institute of Public Affairs

Copy-editing, design, production

E. B. Green Editorial, St. Paul, Minnesota

Printing and binding

Sexton Printing, Inc., St. Paul, and Muscle Bound Bindery, Minneapolis

Contents

Part III
Creating New Institutions

Foreword

The Hubert H. Humphrey Institute of Public Affairs is a special place. On any given day, local, national, or international media will promulgate the ideas, research, or informed opinions of one or more of its talented faculty, fellows, alumni, or students. This is because we at the Humphrey Institute take seriously our obligation to share our work with the public. Our dedication to public education makes the college special.

John Brandl prepared this volume in that spirit. It is an effort to inform the public of a number of policy and planning issues that impact the lives of Americans. Much in this volume is captured from the institute's more than twenty-five years of shared experience in teaching the tools of policy analysis and planning. The approach is to find the common good in the empirical evidence that our analysis produces, to open a dialogue with the community, and to advocate for change if change is needed.

The Humphrey Institute is a living tribute to a man who practiced this form of public education as a political leader—Hubert H. Humphrey. We believe that what we teach in the classroom—the effort we make to inspire and educate young leaders—must extend as well to the public. It is our hope that the articles presented here will serve both to inform and to inspire public dialogue. Vice President Humphrey would want it that way.

I offer special thanks to my predessor, John Brandl, whose own scholarship, community spirit, and appreciation for his colleagues' work inspired this offering. Throughout his career, Professor Brandl has kept one foot in the academy and one in the public arena. As a member of the faculty, he was elected to the Minnesota State Legislature. His superb public service, integrity, and passion for objective analysis make him an ideal role model for Humphrey students. As editor of this volume—and as its inspiration—he continues to perform that role.

John Brandl and the contributors to this book deserve our gratitude. This is a fitting way to commemorate more than twenty-five years of excellence at the Humphrey Institute.

—J. Brian Atwood, Dean
Humphrey Institute of Public Affairs
University of Minnesota

Introduction

On the occasion of the Hubert H. Humphrey Institute of Public Affairs' 25th anniversary in 2002, I envisioned a collection of short essays by institute professors and fellows, each describing an idea of the author that has had a bearing on public affairs. This book is that compilation.

People at the Humphrey Institute (we all call it "the Humphrey") endeavor both to understand how governments function and to improve government policies and operation. The first is necessary for the second. That is, to be of influence, one must comprehend, a fact overlooked by those who fault the academy for concentrating too much on theory and not enough on action. This book is a sampling of the theorizing and action research that go on at the Humphrey, but it is just a sampling. Many more such books could be assembled from the diverse and prolific scholar-practitioners there.

The chapters of Part I describe the generation and testing of conjectures or theories about how five disparate aspects of public affairs function. The remaining essays have to do with influencing policy or management or politics. They fall into two types: those about inventing new techniques for managers or activists (Part II) and those about designing institutions that encourage or direct the behavior of individuals toward public purposes (Part III). Parts II and III illustrate a continuing disagreement—between those citizens and scholars who see improving government as providing knowledge and skills to individuals who are assumed to be public-spirited, and those who understand the task to be devising institutions that induce often self-interested individuals to behave in publicly beneficial ways.

I. Understanding Public Affairs

Universities produce and test ideas—most of them theories about whether and how one thing affects another. Each of the essays in Part I describes the discovery or testing of one such idea. In some cases these ideas remain controversial, which is not unusual in the social sciences.

Testing theories involving human behavior remains more difficult than corresponding efforts in the physical and natural sciences, where it is less common for competing theories to co-exist for extended periods. Much of politics involves such competing theories—the presence of confounding relationships and variables makes difficult the disagreements over matters that are potentially resolvable by careful observation. Think of the continuing dispute over the effect of the capital gains tax on economic growth. Or of the effect of minimum wage on employment, of race on intelligence, or class size on student achievement.

So do not be put off by the lack of final resolution brought to these discussions by Humphrey Institute authors. Each has advanced our understanding and produced a leading—or the leading—explanation of the phenomenon he or she has studied.

Robert Kudrle considers an aspect of globalization, the supposed negative effect of investment coming into a country from elsewhere. Many hold that banning such investment is beneficial to a country. For example, some attributed much of Japan's economic success in the 1970s and 1980s to its apparent ability to keep out foreign companies. Kudrle has looked into the question of whether countries' attempts to inhibit investments from abroad actually work. To everyone's surprise he found that Canada's apparently "ferocious"—his word—attempts to spurn foreign investment into that country from the mid-1970s to the mid-1980s appear to have had little effect on the amount of investment coming to Canada from abroad. He uses his finding to illustrate his conviction that the intentions underlying policies do not automatically translate into results and that, in any event, success is almost always a matter of degree.

An evaluator would quantify that degree. Kudrle sees a world more complicated than we might like and counsels that researchers not overstate their findings. "Qualification," he writes, "must remain a badge of honor."

G. Edward Schuh's proudest academic achievement grew from an insight he gained in answering for himself an examination question he had given to students. Working for two days and nights straight, he concluded that America's becoming the world's banker had had unforeseen deleterious effects on American agriculture. Chronic overvaluation of the dollar explains an extended period of difficulty for U.S. agriculture, because its exports were thereby made more expensive to foreigners, and it fostered the exodus of workers from that industry, all coinciding with remarkable technological advances in that sector of the economy.

Morris Kleiner and his Harvard colleague Richard Freeman set out to determine whether unionization adversely influences a firm's ability to compete and survive. They compared many unionized and non-unionized companies, statistically accounted for other differences between the two groups, and found that, on balance, unionization does not affect a firm's financial health. Counter-examples exist, of course, but the surprising Kleiner-Freeman statistical findings, together with their observation that it is ordinarily not in the interest of a union to bring down a company at which its members work, combine to create an understanding that anyone claiming a relationship between union-ization and diminished competitiveness must now confront.

Understanding the economic geography of metropolitan areas has been the professional preoccupation of John Adams for several decades. He noticed that roads and transit radiating from downtowns not only brought people to work but also provided a direction (roughly out-ward along the radius on which they resided) in which they tended to move when prosperity enabled them to buy better houses. The move-ment outward created concentric rings in which were repeated the characteristics of the original inner-city clusterings: "Working-class sectors in the central city spawned working-class suburbs; elite sec-tors of the central city spawned elite suburbs, and so forth." In recent years he has added to his model of urban development a variety of other influences on where people settle. The resulting insights into the functioning of metropolitan areas have made him one of the world's leading urban geographers.

"Smart growth" is a current movement attracting many people who are concerned about urban sprawl. Its advocates claim that when urban design accomplishes greater population density and pleasant neighborhoods, people in large numbers will turn from driving their cars to walking and using mass transit. Kevin Krizek is favorably dis-posed towards but also skeptical about smart growth. He raises the possibility that large numbers of people simply prefer to drive their own cars regardless of how supposedly attractive urban design may render walking and transit use. Similarly he has identified other factors that confound an easy understanding of what determines the use of cars. Krizek has shown that the link between urban design and the use of automobiles is more complex than smart-growth advocates might wish.

II. Inventing New Techniques for Managers and Activists

While most of the work of the Humphrey Institute researchers just discussed concentrates on understanding the world of public affairs, others are devoted to devising approaches and techniques for improving the practice of policymaking, planning, management, and politics.

In his essay, Harry Boyte describes not a piece of research but a life's work. His ambitious project straddles categories I, II, and III; he theorizes about governance, devises ways to improve the practice of politics, and designs institutions fostering productive public work. Boyte is inventing an alternative to what he calls the ideological wars of contemporary politics.

In the latter form of politics the modus operandi is to identify a person or group associated with an unwanted policy, then calumniate the opponent to discredit the policy. Instead, drawing on the American tradition of commonwealth, Boyte understands politics as drawing disparate groups into respectful negotiation over how best to accomplish their several desires, then doing what he calls the "real work"—carrying out the necessary tasks. Thousands of people with whom he has worked, ranging from nursing-home residents to elementary school students to new immigrants to groups composed of Protestants and Catholics in Northern Ireland, have demonstrated the efficacy of his approach. Public Achievement, an organization he formed to encourage this type of politics, is thriving now in scores of American communities and eleven other countries.

John Bryson is perhaps the country's leading academician in the field of strategic planning for governmental and nonprofit organizations. He writes that his work is to help people "determine what they want, how to get it, and why." His contributions include inventing a model that practitioners may use to accomplish an array of work from defining a mission and developing a plan to assembling a coalition of people to assure the plan's acceptance and implementation.

For two decades the Humphrey Institute's Reflective Leadership Center, two of whose directors were Robert Terry and Barbara Crosby, was a base both for inventing leadership techniques and for testing their efficacy. Their innovations included construing a broad array of the populace as leaders, identifying appropriate leadership actions for particular needs of organizations, and linking leadership to ethics. Legions of participants testify to the powerful effect that the Reflective Leadership Center has had on their lives.

Ann Markusen's research reported here supports a policy agenda, namely conversion of military resources to other public purposes. Her contribution has been to learn and teach how that conversion can take place. She recognizes national-security requirements but works out their opportunity costs in terms of other public benefits foregone. She identifies military expenditures driven more by political pressure than by their contribution to national defense. And she forges partnerships for mutual learning and for making the case for the policy agenda.

Lee Munnich describes one research effort that he and his colleagues in the Humphrey's State and Local Policy Program have conducted. They applied the idea of industry clusters (the self-encouraging agglomeration that sometimes occurs among firms in related types of business) to the Twin Cities region and then to rural Minnesota. They identified the most important industry groups, made some predictions about their future directions (for example, they anticipated the merger of large banks several years before Norwest merged with Wells Fargo and First Banks with U.S. Bank), and gave numerous communities an understanding of where their best economic prospects lay.

While he was co-director of the Humphrey Institute's Conflict and Change Center, Thomas Fiutak devised an aid for mediators, a model for mediation. He construes mediation as a form of assisted negotiation, showing practitioners the stages through which to guide a mediation and the actions to take when participating groups reach an impasse. He has demonstrated and taught his model in innumerable situations across the United States and in many other countries.

III. Creating New Institutions

Some of the scholars whose work is described in the previous section implicitly assume that those for whom they devise improved techniques will regularly use them in the public interest. (The Humphrey Institute is, after all, a school whose students we hope will go on to accomplish public good.) But many at the Humphrey understand the challenge of governance to be the construction of arrangements that lead sometimes self-interested people to act in socially productive ways. They concentrate not on educating individuals but on redesigning institutions that shape the behavior of individuals.

In the decade and a half since the demise of the Soviet Union and its dominion over neighboring countries, Humphrey Institute representatives, led by Zbigniew Bochniarz, have worked in about a dozen countries in that part of the world. Their efforts began with the design of market-based incentives for bringing about environmental improvement. (Many Communist regimes generated massive environmental problems; in some central and eastern European countries environmental groups were the only significant forces other than the church to confront government.) Over the years Bochniarz and his colleagues, through the Humphrey's Center for Nations in Transition, have assisted in the formation of a score of environmental research and action groups, postdiploma study programs in governance and management, and national blueprints for environmental improvement, sustainable development, and management education.

The emphasis has been on the design of legislation, governmental institutions, nonprofit organizations, and university curricula to orient the behavior of individuals toward socially beneficial behavior.

Bochniarz asserts with good reason: "The Humphrey Institute . . . is the leader among U.S. universities facilitating the historical transformation from centrally planned economies with totalitarian political regimes to civic societies with liberal economies."

Marsha Freeman writes of the International Women's Rights Action Watch, a Humphrey Institute Center created by Arvonne Fraser and subsequently led first by Fraser, then by Freeman. IWRAW was a network of individuals around the world who detected, investigated, and confronted injustice against women. IWRAW was perhaps unique. Linked to the United Nations, it was extra-governmental. While it was composed of individuals linked strongly enough to constitute an international force, each participant could take actions appropriate to her or his country's circumstances, her actions supported but not determined by a central office. IWRAW became "the global operations and resource center for work on [a treaty subscribed to by 180 countries,] the Convention on the Elimination of All Forms of Discrimination Against Women."

My own professional preoccupation, included in Part III, is the "governance question"—how can a free people induce its members regularly to act not merely self-interestedly but in socially beneficial ways? Inattention to this question explains the weakness of much government policy that implicitly assumes that appropriations will be put to best use, that civil servants and others administering policy will spontaneously seek the public good. I understand policymaking to be the design of arrangements that motivate and provide incentives to people in ways that make their personal interests coincide with public interests. For much of what government does—the delivery of services—acceptable quality may be expected only if service producers are subject to competition or are members of communities so strong that they draw individuals regularly to act for the welfare of others.

Nancy Eustis is a leader of the national transformation in how government provides services to the elderly and to persons with disabilities. Only a generation ago it was generally thought appropriate for such services to be organized and produced by assumedly well-meaning governmental and nonprofit authorities for delivery to passive recipients. Eustis and her colleagues, concerned that such practice was inherently both costly and disrespectful of recipients, have devised alternative models in which recipients make the basic decisions concerning the services they will receive and who will provide them. Empowering people with choice is respectful, is at least potentially cost-effective, and constitutes a way of holding service providers accountable.

Joe Nathan directs the Humphrey Institute's Center for School Change. He and his colleagues study and encourage the development of alternatives to the dominant organizational form within which elementary and secondary education is now conducted—namely, monopoly bureaucracies in which employees receive pay and perquisites whether the children learn or not. Nathan has been as influential as anyone in the country in bringing a variety of choice arrangements to public education, arrangements in which families decide which school and type of education is best for their children. One such arrangement, invented by Nathan and a few colleagues, is charter schools. These are public schools whose continued existence depends on their meeting the conditions of the agreement or charter—what funds they will receive and what educational results they will achieve.

Conclusion

The myriad activities at the Humphrey Institute follow no disciplinary, ideological, or partisan agenda. The people here have in common the conviction that thinking helps. Research can yield improvements both in our understanding of public affairs and in how public policy may advance the common good. We hope the essays that follow give readers insight into what people at the Humphrey do and why they are proud of their work.

Part I

Understanding Public Affairs

—1—

A U.S. Policy Change
Leads to a Surprising Discovery about Canada

Robert Kudrle

The American economic landscape appeared very different to most of us fifteen years ago from how it does today. We now face a multitude of challenges connected with what is almost invariably called globalization. And some issues that then commanded attention have disappeared or been moved to the back burner. For example, flagging U.S. productivity growth riveted people's attention and provided planks for political platforms as late as the early 1990s in a way that is now hard to imagine.

But the biggest change almost certainly lies in our reactions to Japan. When students of today's Hubert H. Humphrey Institute of Public Affairs were in grade school, this nation had experienced the evaporation of Soviet power and not yet considered the implications of unprecedented growth rates in a state as large as China. Neither had it considered, despite the Gulf War, the international implications of clashes between tradition and modernization in the Muslim world. We were almost transfixed by the apparently unstoppable Japanese juggernaut that had supplanted American output in important economic sectors through exportation and apparently was consolidating its grip by massive investment in the United States.

How times change! By the mid-1990s, Japan's economic pause was seen as a real crisis, and that crisis has largely continued with only tentative signs of substantial improvement. This situation is utterly without parallel in economic history. Unlike the U.S. depression of the 1930s, the Japanese economy did not collapse—it just stopped growing.

Public and private U.S. policymakers in the 1980s and early 1990s reacted to Japan in predictable ways. Those practices that could be imitated were embraced; those that could not, were decried. All kinds of management techniques fell into the former category, while the latter included explicit and implicit trade barriers. The Japanese also had a long history of severely limiting foreign direct investment (FDI), a practice they claimed largely to have abandoned. The murkiness of Japanese decision-making and the extremely low level of foreign operations in Japan, however, led many Americans to believe that the Japanese continued to discourage FDI.

Many people also believed that curtailing FDI from abroad played a central role in Japanese economic success. During 1988 deliberations over the legislation authorizing U.S. participation in the Uruguay Round of trade liberalization under the General Agreement on Tariffs and Trade (GATT), some in Congress advocated granting the president a veto over foreign investment in the United States that might threaten its "economic security." This apparently almost unlimited discretion was modified to read "national security" before the legislation passed. As critics then noted, however, no definitions of either term were offered. An activist president appeared to have the authority to block virtually anything—without Congressional or judicial review.

No one knew just what to make of the new presidential power embodied in the "Exon-Florio Amendment." Some shrugged it off as a gesture. Others believed its presence would have a "chilling effect" on the generally welcome FDI boom of the 1980s, which came far more from Europe and Canada than from Japan.

I had studied foreign direct investment and its institutional embodiment—"the multinational corporation"—for my doctoral dissertation and through all of the years since then. For years I had taught a course on the subject at the Humphrey Institute. And I was interested in the possible effects of Exon-Florio.

Although my first instinct was to look for a foreign situation analogous to that of the United States, I knew that finding a close parallel would be impossible. Until the 1980s, "the multinational corporation" was essentially global shorthand for "U.S. business abroad." We looked at the subject from an entirely different perspective than did the rest of the world.

Most economists, including me, believed that such activity was generally positive for the "host" country and, despite the misgivings reflected in Exon-Florio, that U.S. policies still left foreigners facing less hindrance than those of virtually any other country. The world, moreover, was zigging while the United States was zagging. A global confluence of ideological change, evidence, and fad had generated a massive shift to markets in rich and poor countries alike by the mid-1980s. Nearly all states were reducing their controls over FDI, and many were actively recruiting FDI as never before.

Was the mere existence of Exon-Florio likely to have a negative effect on the flow of FDI into the United States? I saw one place to look for clues—in our neighbor Canada. The necessary research also addressed the unexplored issue of Canadian investment screening, which I had considered examining even before the Exon-Florio issue arose.

Political sociologists regard the United States and Canada as "most similar systems." I had explored many similarities as well as differences in earlier work (with Theodore Marmor) on the development of the welfare state in the two countries. But it doesn't take a social scientist to identify the major difference between the two countries: the asymmetry in their influence on each other, which in turn rests largely on the fact that in many economic dimensions, the United States is about ten times the size of Canada. Canada's decreased policy discrimination in favor of Britain over the early postwar decades brought increasing U.S. economic dominance in trade and FDI. By the early 1970s Canada had a much higher level of foreign industrial ownership than any other large developed country.

The Trudeau government, acting on the basis of several government reviews, decided that foreign investors, particularly from the United States, were dominating the Canadian economy to an unacceptable degree. Parliament passed legislation establishing the Foreign Investment Review Agency (FIRA). The agency began evaluating takeovers in 1974 and startups in 1975. A decade later the Canadian government, afraid that its reputation of hostility towards foreign investment was contributing to its weak overall economic performance, changed the name of the agency to Investment Canada. It gave nearly all foreign investment a green light and devoted more resources to attracting foreign investment than to screening it.

Official figures on the book value of foreign investment in Canada suggest the Canadians acted long after the problem was most severe. Those data, obtained from firms, indicate that the share of foreign ownership reached its apogee before World War II and declined steadily during the postwar period.

But there were important reasons for not taking those figures seriously. Perpetual postwar inflation meant that company books tended systematically to undervalue plant and equipment by recording them at their acquisition price and reducing them each year with a depreciation formula. I was fortunate to have access to an investment value-estimation technique recently developed by Profs. Robert Eisner and

Paul Pieper (the U.S. Department of Commerce has since adopted it). After reconstructing the data with this technique, I calculated that the U.S. share of total Canadian capital grew over the entire postwar period—by 160 percent between 1950 and 1960 and by another 106 percent to 1973. Using this same reconstructed series, FIRA's restrictiveness showed up as impressive; the subsequent growth through 1987 was only 41 percent.

While it certainly appeared that FIRA had a strong effect, multivariate statistical techniques could help sort out the varied influences on incoming U.S. investment and show the apparent effect of the agency's role while holding other factors constant. This was not easy. In examining somewhat comparable studies, I found about a dozen variables demanding inclusion, and many of them admitted to alternative operationalizations. Even the treatment of the FIRA effect could be considered in several ways. The necessity for including in the analysis both the existence of the screening process and the rate at which projects were approved became clear.

To make a long story short, once various formulations were tested, the evidence for any substantial systematic FIRA effect on investment flows into Canada came into doubt. Moreover, one apparent implication of the screening of investments and associated bargaining, namely reduced profitability, could not be detected. How could this be? FIRA declined a higher rate of proposals, in some years as high as 30 percent or more, than any similar agency in the world. How could such apparently vigorous screening not show up in reduced flows of FDI?

There were candidate answers. My 1995 article based on this research, "The Foreign Investment Review Agency and U.S. Direct Investment in Canada," *Transnational Corporations* 4(2), makes clear that some data limitations, particularly confining the study to U.S. investment, may have biased the results (though there was indirect evidence that this was not the case). More important, FIRA projected a somewhat misleading impression of its work. Many of the proposals that FIRA rejected (even after bargaining) were reformulated and came back at least once more before approval. But because the extent of this resubmission was little known, it did not help Canada's poor image with direct investors. This bad image was, after all, one of the main reasons the government changed the agency's name to Investment Canada in 1985.

A real possibility for explanation is that FIRA functioned mainly at the level of political symbolism. It reassured the public, which had strong concerns about foreign domination, without much additional effect.

What conclusion does this piece of research warrant?

First, ideas may take on lives of their own without much factual basis, even when evidence to challenge what has become myth is available. The history of myths shows that they may be composed of truth and falsehood in nearly any combination. I may not have completely dispelled the myth that FIRA was a serious impediment to U.S. investment in Canada, but I certainly examined it as nobody had done before. Given the prominence of the subject in Canadian policy circles, I still find this amazing.

Second, some myths, such as the one examined here, largely concern quantity, and, when they do, quantitative analysis must be brought to bear. Nearly all of what I did in this research employed tools taught to all Humphrey Institute students then and to most of them now. But the claims of myth—and, more broadly, the relation of policy to outcomes—almost always combine qualitative and quantitative elements. Because we can often nail down the quantitative part of a problem fairly well, that part may receive more emphasis than it deserves. Nonetheless, those skeptical of quantitative work often take more comfort in *that* truth than is warranted.

The research strongly questioned FIRA's impact on the volume of investment. It even more strongly challenged FIRA's impact on profitability. Those defending the agency's performance have the choice of reanalyzing the quantitative data (although a subsequent study done by others came to conclusions similar to mine) or of making a case for the positive impact in other dimensions, a challenge nobody appears to have taken up.

Third, we must examine data carefully. Sociologists often accuse economists of neglecting data quality because greater attention could cast doubt on conclusions drawn from fancy econometrics performed on bad numbers. The present research illustrates that problem. Official data in both the United States and Canada are typically as carefully and professionally gathered as any in the world. Nevertheless, we must investigate inadequacies (those in charge of gathering data usually acknowledge them) and face them squarely. In the present case, the failure of official data to correct properly for inflation led to systematic biases that required a radical revision to overcome. The results of earlier research on FIRA's impact, competently performed but based on biased data, were misleading.

Fourth, we must not oversimplify or over-interpret results. Academic social scientists are often criticized, sometimes ridiculed, for the endless qualifications with which they present their conclusions. But the alternative is much worse. To the challenge "Why don't you just say it?" the honest response is often: "The 'it' can be compressed and summarized only so far without distortion." Memorable sound bites, in particular, typically involve such distortion. Qualification must remain a badge of honor.

Finally, lessons learned in one arena may be suggestive elsewhere. My research on FIRA led me to doubt that the Exon-Florio Amendment would result in a detectable effect on direct investment into the United States. That would probably remain true even if the screening were based on a broader construction of national security than any president has yet embraced—or probably ever will. I have conducted research recently that confirms the first part of the hunch. But that is another story.

—2—

The Macroeconomics of Agriculture

G. Edward Schuh

In May 1973, I was delivering the final lecture in a course on inter-national agricultural development at Purdue University. It was a graduate-level course—most of the students were doctoral candidates.

An important feature of the economic environment at that time was an upward spiral of commodity prices. This was a conundrum at the time, for agricultural commodity prices had been drifting down-ward for a long while. My lecture was on economic policy, especially on macroeconomic policy and how it affects agricultural development. I explained to the class that policymakers in the developing countries tended to discriminate against agriculture by shifting the price of ag commodities down relative to those in the rest of the economy. (That ratio of prices is referred to as the *domestic terms of trade*.) The policy instruments used for this purpose accorded high levels of protection to the manufacturing sector, through a gamut of explicit export taxes primarily affecting the agricultural sector—and implicit export taxes in the form of greatly overvalued currency values.

I went on to explain that the overvaluation of currency typically is not an explicit goal of policymakers, but a condition they fall into by failing to devalue their currencies in response to changing economic conditions. The point is that policymakers fear devaluations of their currency because such realignments are typically associated with a surge in domestic rates of inflation, especially in food and energy prices. Urban populations are especially vulnerable to such increases in prices and tended to be politically volatile.

As I was explaining this phenomenon, I suddenly realized it was precisely the problem faced by the United States at that time. For the first time in decades, the country had in 1971 devalued the dollar, as a means to end its chronic balance-of-payments problem. Devaluing the dollar was expected to increase U.S. exports by making the external price cheaper in terms of other currencies and to reduce American imports by making the domestic prices of such goods and services more expensive.

This first realignment did not have much immediate impact on the balance of payments, however, since realignments in currency values typically take up to eighteen months to have much of an effect. Hence, the dollar was devalued again in 1973, set free to float in response to changing economic conditions. The U.S. monetary authorities announced that henceforth the value of the dollar would be whatever the market for currencies said it was worth.

My thought was that putting that observation in the form of a question on the final exam would be an excellent test of the students' understanding of much of the material covered in the course. I returned to my office at the end of class and wrote down the question, lest I forget it. Typically, I tried to write the answer to my question to be sure it was feasible.

I became intrigued with the answer and worked steadily for forty-eight hours—without taking a break—writing a paper to work out the details. Many things suddenly became clear to me about U.S. agriculture, both over time and in the contemporary world. I suddenly realized that the U.S. dollar had been the world's currency for some time and that the world was on the equivalent of a dollar standard. I also realized that the situation prevailed through a persistent overvaluation of the dollar. That meant that the U.S. agricultural sector, one of our leading export sectors, was persistently taxed by an overvalued currency. I began to trace the history of this process and argued that the farm crisis of the 1950s was in part due to this policy.

My analysis did not stop there. I adopted a model of induced technological change and used it to understand why the pace of technological change had been so rapid in the agricultural sector, despite discrimination against the sector on the part of policymakers. Other dimensions of U.S. agricultural development also became clear, such as the role of the market in expulsing and subsidizing the exodus of excess labor from the sector. As I worked, my excitement with the material (and with my conclusions) grew.

When finished with the paper two days later, I sent it off to the editor of the *American Journal of Agricultural Economics* and then got some sleep. The editor was so interested in the paper that he phoned to say the journal would publish it without review. Explaining the paper's genesis and that I had not even passed it by my colleagues, I suggested he do both him and me a favor and have it reviewed. He agreed and sent it to four reviewers. Three of them were almost as enthusiastic about the paper as the editor and I. The fourth delayed in responding. Finally, the editor phoned me to suggest that I take care of the minor suggestions made by the reviewers and send it in. He wanted to get it published!

I made the changes and was about to send it off in final form. About that time he received a letter from the fourth reviewer. That person, who signed his name even though he was not required to, responded with one sentence: "This trash doesn't merit journal space!"

The editor told me to pay the comment no mind, and he published the paper with the title "The Exchange Rate and U.S. Agriculture" (February 1974, pp. 1–13). Thus began a new way of thinking about agricultural policy and the development of agriculture. The American Agricultural Economics Association each year gives an award for the best article in its journal. The article won the award in 1975. Each year the association also gives an award to the published research of most lasting value—over the previous ten years. The article won that award as well.

That paper, and the insights it carried, led to a great deal of additional research and publication and to a new way of thinking about agriculture—about how it relates to the remainder of the general economy and about the role of macroeconomic policy as it affects the sector. I presented a plenary paper—"The New Macroeconomics of Agriculture"—at the annual meeting of the American Agricultural Economics Association (AAEA) a couple of years later. Still later, when I was invited to give the Fellows Address at an annual meeting of the AAEA, I discussed the issue of optimal currency areas and the implications for international relations. (This series of papers resulted in my eventually receiving the association's award for outstanding policy work.) Later I was commissioned to do a contribution on "The Macroeconomics of Agriculture" for the *Encyclopedia of the Social Sciences.*

Especially rewarding was the large amount of empirical research engendered by the article among others. The idea that the value of the nation's currency mattered was relatively new to the U.S. academic and policy community. Agricultural economics had grown up with a microeconomic perspective and seldom considered the importance of macroeconomic policies. My good fortune was to have taken my doctoral training at the University of Chicago, where monetarist and Nobel Laureate Milton Friedman held sway intellectually with Nobel Laureate Theodore W. Schultz, who dominated the agricultural-development literature with his perspectives on technological change, education, and the new household economics.

What I learned there was to think differently about things and not necessarily to go with the crowd. (Seven professors with whom I studied later received the Nobel Prize in Economics.) It was also my good fortune to work in developing countries early in my career, especially in Brazil—a country leading in the practice of import-substituting industrialization. This was a field rich in the macroeconomic aspects of economic-development policy.

While there was a lot of disagreement with the insights in my original article, there is little doubt today that the distortions in foreign-exchange markets make a difference or that policymakers must pay attention to their own macroeconomic policies as well as to those of other countries. Ironically, policymakers in the United States still lag in understanding these issues, especially the interactions among monetary policy, financial flows, the value of our currency, and sectoral policy. For example, U.S. agriculture was plagued for much of the past decade, its problem rooted in a strong dollar. At the same time, we experienced similar problems with the steel industry, also rooted in the strong dollar. For the steel industry, the strong dollar has been equivalent to a subsidy on imports. In neither case have U.S. policymakers recognized the cause of the problem and so designed appropriate adjustment policies.

The problem is at least two-dimensional. First, throughout the post-World War II period the United States has been the central banker for the world, and the world has been on a dollar standard. We thus have a tendency to think about a world in which other countries must adjust to our economic policies, rather than our adjusting to theirs. The prevalence of the Breton Woods fixed-exchange-rate system for such a long period contributed to this perspective. Second, and perhaps more important, we still live in a world in which policymakers mostly choose to ignore the recommendations of social scientists, especially economists.

An important challenge of the Humphrey Institute is to do the multidisciplinary research that helps us understand why policymakers do what they do (or don't do!). William Ascher attempted to answer that question in his book *Why Governments Waste Natural Resources: Policy Failures in Developing Countries* (John Hopkins University Press, 1999). His argument is that policymakers tend to respond to their own policy agenda and policy goals, not to the efficiency-dominated, objective function of the economists. If the Humphrey, with its impressive array of talent, is to contribute to improving the lives of all people—both here and abroad—we must with our collective mind attempt an understanding of why policymakers do what they do. That will require multidisciplinary collaboration on a scale we have not experienced in the past.

—3—

Analysis and the Public-Policy Process: Union Effects on Firm Survival

Morris M. Kleiner

Does unionization affect a company's chances for survival? One summer a union leader attending the Harvard Trade Union program mentioned to me and the distinguished labor economist Richard Freeman that one of the toughest challenges that union organizers face is the threat by management to close a plant or move it offshore. He explained that even though such a threat is illegal under the National Labor Relations Act, statements by senior management that a union-ized business will close cause many workers to fear union organizing at their workplace.

The union official then asked whether there was any analysis of the effects of unionization on a firm's survival. Neither of us knew of any study that could answer his question about whether unionization threatened a company's solvency. After some discussion with the union official, Professor Freeman and I thought we could develop a method to examine these management threats using data from companies or data gathered on workers by the federal government.

Analyzing the Question

After reviewing information on this issue in some detail, we thought it would take considerable time and money to find a factually based answer to his question. Given the limitations of the data available from published sources, we decided to mimic a scientifically based experiment as closely as possible. This approach meant gathering information available from publicly traded firms still in business, as well as from ones that were defunct or had declared bankruptcy. We would then attempt to compile economic and organizational characteristics for all of them.

Following some efforts to determine how we could obtain data on the experimental group (companies that were union-organized) and the control group (companies that were not union-organized), we submitted a proposal for funding to the U.S. National Science Foundation (NSF). In a detailed peer-review process, experts on social science methods reviewed and evaluated our proposed study.

Given the controversial nature of the project, which had skeptics in both labor- and management-interest groups, we were uncertain about whether a federal agency like the NSF would support a study carrying a risk of animosity from these two powerful political constituencies. To our delight, following some minor revisions to our methodological approach, we were successful in obtaining funding that included support for graduate students from the Humphrey Institute to do much of the data gathering, which included calling firms and unions.

Over the next three years, five students were funded for all or part of their graduate studies at the institute from this grant. Three of them wrote master's papers based on the data gathered from the study. This allowed them to finish graduation requirements earlier than they had anticipated. One student working on the project, Janet Bull, received the Lloyd B. Short Award for the best master's paper written at the Humphrey in 1989. Another, Mohan Ramanujan, obtained full-time employment with the prestigious National Bureau of Economic Research (NBER), based in part on the analysis completed in his paper.

After gathering survey data and other information from publicly available sources, we analyzed the data using methods that statistically account for factors that may result in differences between the experimental group and the control groups. What were the results? The statistical analysis found that unions do not help or harm the ability of firms to survive. Moreover, contrary to the statements often made by management, firms with unions or organizing drives are on average no more likely to suffer financial difficulty, or to engage in large-scale layoffs, than organizations without unions.

Although unionized firms are somewhat less profitable than non-union firms, unions sometimes serve as a way for companies to pay higher-than-average wages during good times, but to take back many of the benefits during business-cycle contractions. The AFL's first president, Samuel Gompers, suggested that "the worst crime against working people is a company that fails to operate at a profit." Unions know this. Further, they are not usually foolish enough to kill the goose that lays the golden egg. Although unions, like companies, make mistakes that harm a company and their own members, they are no more likely than management to do so.

After developing several versions of our analysis, we produced a working paper published by the NBER in Cambridge, Massachusetts. This organization is the most widely respected, nonpartisan economic-research organization, and it is highly influential in providing studies of how the economy works. As an illustration of the impact of NBER working papers, currently about six thousand of its research papers are downloaded daily from its Web site.

Following the listing of the study by the NBER, references and summaries of the paper began showing up in many of the major newspapers in the United States. For example, the *New York Times* summarized the study in a feature article published August 31, 1997, titled "On Payday Union Jobs Stack Up Well." Also, the study was examined in the *Wall Street Journal* in an article published on May 30, 1991, titled "Recovery May Not Help the Labor Unions." The findings also became the basis of an editorial examining the costs and benefits of unions in the United States, titled "Properly Run, Unions Give Workers More Voice and Higher Pay" and published in the (Minneapolis) *Star Tribune* on April 21, 1996.

Minnesota Public Radio asked me to comment on the labor movement's impact on businesses on an hour-long program on Labor Day on September 7, 1998. Many major union papers then picked up on the story as a feature. A union-member friend of my father pointed out the story, reprinted from the *New York Times* article mentioned above in a Peoria, Illinois, regional union paper, while they were on their morning walk.

A major goal of the National Science Foundation in its funding of the project was to inform the academic community, and thereby students in the social sciences and policy programs, about the role of unions in modern democratic societies. After a review process requiring analysis of the paper by additional experts in labor, the study titled "Do Unions Make Enterprises Insolvent?" appeared as the lead—commonly viewed as the best—paper in the July 1999 *Industrial and Labor Relations Review.* This publication, generally regarded as the premier journal in labor and industrial relations, draws the widest readership in the field. As a consequence, this revised version of the study was widely downloaded from the Social Science Research Network.

Public-Policy Impacts

One difficult yet rewarding challenge of being in a public-policy school is the dual goal of meeting the high scholarly standards of the academic community and having an impact on the policy debate for central issues in one's field. In this case, I was able to do both. As a consequence of both the academic and general media attention this study received, Prof. John Dunlop (former Secretary of Labor, chair of the Presidential Commission on the Future of Labor-Management Relations, and now deceased) cited our findings in the commission's report to the president and to Congress in 1994.

One measure of the effect of these studies is that they continue to have an impact. In the fall of 2002, Senator Ted Kennedy and Senator Paul Wellstone (now deceased) sponsored Senate hearings examining the impact of unions in the economy. Several individuals, including my coauthor Richard Freeman, some leaders of the labor movement, and experts in labor relations, were invited to testify. They often referred to our study as evidence that unions do not contribute to firm insolvency or to major layoffs in the workplace. Union organizers and policy advocates in the labor movement now can note that assertions that an organization will close as result of a union-organizing drive are illegal, and that they not supported by the best available statistical evidence. In this study we achieved an outcome that resulted in both academic acceptability and policy relevance.

In conclusion, one of the unique aspects of the Humphrey is its focus on the interaction of academics and practitioners and their mutual learning. Unlike many departments in which the goal is primarily the advancement of an academic discipline, public-policy programs seek both to advance scholarship and to inform public policies. Consequently, faculty members of the Humphrey Institute must meet the highest standards of the academy while influencing the world of public affairs. This case illustrates how beneficial these interactions can be for all the principals involved.

—4—

Metropolitan Housing Submarkets
and Public Policy

John S. Adams

I read somewhere that coming up with a new and insightful idea isn't too difficult. What's hard is to take a promising idea and accomplish something with it. One idea I have worked with for many years concerns the nature of *geographically defined housing submarkets* in metropolitan areas—how they originate, how they work, and how an understanding of their operation can and should directly influence metropolitan planning and housing policy and indirectly affect state as well as local fiscal policy.

Background
The idea of geographically defined housing submarkets—that is, submarkets defined in terms of their spatial (or geographical) extent rather than in terms of market segmentation based on price, floor area, num-

ber of rooms, style, age, structural characteristics, and so forth—first dawned on me in the 1960s as I was completing my doctoral research and starting a new round of investigations.

At that time, regional economists and economic geographers focused mainly on questions of industrial production and the economic transitions underway in declining (Appalachia, for example) as well as booming (California, for example) regions of the United States after World War II. This emphasis on production was a legacy of the depression years of the 1930s, when President Franklin Roosevelt and his economic advisers faced the question of how to crank up a stagnant national economy.

National economic life was improving by the last years of the 1930s, and World War II provided a further stimulus. But after the war, attention to problems accompanying uneven economic development continued as major surges in some sectors (for example, automobiles, defense, and steel) showered benefits on the regions producing them and their inputs even as sharp declines occurred simultaneously in the upland South and some other parts of the country. Massive population movements from the South to manufacturing centers in the Northeast and West, plus the steady movements of surplus labor from mechanized farms to cities, accompanied the economic shifts.

At the local level, the study of cities, metropolitan areas, and larger urban-centered regions by social scientists was still in its infancy in the 1950s. But suburban expansion, central city decline, and the interstate highway program presented dramatic challenges. The federal Housing Act of 1949 provided significant federal money for inner-city slum clearance and urban renewal, but the theoretical foundations upon which urban renewal and public housing programs rested were seriously flawed. Professional planning practice focused primarily on physical design. Experts trained as architects and engineers, lacking sufficient knowledge of urban geography and economics, guided the planning and rebuilding of America's inner cities. Land-use zoning persisted as the primary mechanism for allocating urban land to various uses, for separating nuisances from high-quality residential neighborhoods, and often for maintaining socioeconomic segregation within cities and ensuring the homogeneity of their flourishing suburbs.

While economic and demographic landscapes were being reshaped on national and local scales, a series of prominent regional economic-development studies got underway in the 1950s and 1960s with government and private foundation support. Their aim was to assess what was happening; their hope, to figure out what could be done from a public-policy standpoint to improve things. These initiatives were undertaken before the U.S. Supreme Court in 1962 decided *Baker v. Carr* ("one man, one vote"), so over-represented rural interests usually supported them with enthusiasm. They focused on regions centered by New York City, Philadelphia, Pittsburgh, St. Louis, Appalachia, as well as on the Ninth Federal Reserve District (cf. The Upper Midwest Economic Study).

My Epiphany

Two jobs that I held during my graduate school years set the stage for my housing-market research. The first was work as a research assistant on the Upper Midwest Economic Study (1960–64) at the University of Minnesota, and the second was my dissertational research (1964–66). The former effort acquainted me with available theories and policy measures that might bear on describing and analyzing major American regions undergoing significant economic and demographic change after World War II. The dissertation project focused on how those regional shifts played out with respect to the allocation (and persistence) of urban land for industrial use inside the Minneapolis area.

When my thoughts turned to what I might publish from my dissertation work, it dawned on me that the production side of urban life—how a city and the people in it earn their living, by what processes urban land is allocated for production, why land-use arrangements persist long after they become obsolete—formed only part of the story. The other part was the consumption side of urban life—how people spend their money and time, what they do when they are not at work, how land is allocated for consumption and leisure.

This reflection led me to observe that the single largest user of urban land is housing. I went on to discover, believe it or not, that there was almost no contemporary literature by historians, geographers, economists, or other social scientists on the subject of urban housing in America! That seemed an open invitation to work on the topic, and so I began.

A Research Program

The thinking that led to a research plan for studying the geography of metropolitan housing markets took three directions.

First, I began exploring selected aspects of the *demand side* of urban housing markets from a geographical standpoint, namely the search-and-selection process undertaken by a household in acquiring new or different housing.

I observed that from 1890 until the 1960s, most movement in cities had been radial, that is, in–and–out, between peripheral residential neighborhoods and the central business district (CBD) for work, shopping, and entertainment. Streetcar and bus lines provided the principal movement options, and the radial lines that focused on the CBD not only channeled residents' daily activity orbits but also limited the opportunity for widening those orbits. Cross-town movement on public transportation in most cities was difficult, time-consuming, and usually unnecessary. One consequence of these daily movement patterns was that urban residents ended up knowing their own section of the city, while the remainder of the city remained essentially *terra incognita.*

I hypothesized, therefore, that when households decided for whatever reason to change their residences to different houses or apartments, they conducted their searches and selections from among known or easily knowable options. I tested these ideas and produced a series of widely cited papers.

Second, I looked at *housing supply* from a geographical standpoint and examined ways that variations in supply produced successive rings of residential expansion around the edges of previously built-up areas, like growth rings on a tree, with each ring expressing faithfully the economic and demographic circumstances extant during the expansion period. It wasn't a sophisticated idea, drawn as it was by analogy from physical geography and how natural forces shape the physical landscape. But this was a time of rising interest in urban housing, and my study was widely noted.

My third line of inquiry brought demand and supply together to explain how the character of *sector-based urban housing submarkets*—working and lower-middle class, middle-class, upper-middle class, and elite—evolved and perpetuated themselves and their respective internal characters.

I based my work partly on studies carried out in the 1930s by real-estate economist Homer Hoyt and partly on later work by geographer David Ward. The main idea was that each residential sector developed a distinctive character in the immigrant and nativist neighborhoods that clustered around the principal activity areas of the CBD at the end of the nineteenth century. With the passage of time and as the city economy and population expanded, sector populations grew with their purchasing power. The *upward* socioeconomic mobility of households was translated into geographic mobility *outward*—to newer and better housing and neighborhoods. As households pushed outward, they carried their tastes and purchasing power with them, and the market responded by building to their tastes and delivering retail goods and services that matched their wants and needs.

Over time, working-class sectors in the central city spawned working-class suburbs; elite sectors of the central city spawned elite suburbs, and so forth. By the final decades of the twentieth century those tendencies had been significantly diluted, but an eighty-year legacy of these market tendencies is easily demonstrated for all major American cities—from New York, Los Angeles and Chicago, to the Twin Cities, Des Moines, and smaller urban areas.

Policy Analysis

Metropolitan housing markets and the geographical submarkets they contain are complex events, not amenable to easy economic analysis, not easily understood by human geographers unlearned in economics, and a complete mystery to planners whose backgrounds are usually in design and landscape architecture. Even real-estate professionals for whom I have offered continuing education courses, regular lectures, and study tours of the Twin Cities are generally unaware of the larger economic and demographic forces and geographic constraints that regulate the neighborhoods in which they sell. Their emphasis is usually on the individual house and neighborhood—what geographers term *site features*—rather than on *situation* or *relative location* in terms of events, trends, forces, and features of settings beyond the site that affect outcomes there.

Understanding the internal dynamics of urban housing markets as a series of geographically defined, sector-oriented submarkets also helps to clarify certain policy analyses. For example, why did urban riots occur at specific locations within cities in the late 1960s and not somewhere else? Or why did minority ghettoes develop in the inner precincts of the most active middle-class housing submarkets after 1920 in most large American cities—for example, in the near-north side as well as directly south of the CBD in Minneapolis and west of the St. Paul Cathedral and Ramsey Hill in St. Paul? Why did house prices fluctuate in different ways within the same metropolitan area?

A review of housing policies at the federal, state, and local levels reveals little understanding of the geographical dynamics of urban housing markets, despite the definition and deployment of policy after policy to fix things. But there is no doubt that the operation of urban housing markets is responsible for many of the difficulties faced by local governments. The federal and state subsidies concentrated in middle-class and upper-middle-class housing sectors produce wealth effects yielding benefits for municipalities lying in their paths, while less-well-endowed sectors and the cities in their paths struggle to pay their bills.

In unrecognized ways, housing policy forms an important element of state and local fiscal policy. Recognition of this reality makes it clear, from a social-justice standpoint, that benefits for some lucky homeowners at certain locations in metropolitan areas come partially at the expense of less-fortunately-located homeowners, landlords, and tenants. Every metropolitan area is a functioning system held together by innumerable structures, flows, and dependencies. But within that system there is considerable imbalance, which leads to tension, unearned gains, and uncompensated losses.

In the past thirty years, I have studied these topics, sometimes with a focus on the Minneapolis-St. Paul area and sometimes by means of comparative analyses of more than two dozen major American metropolitan areas. Today it seems a natural and sensible thing to recognize that each neighborhood and each metropolitan municipality is part of a unified whole and that events in one place (for example, subsidies for new housing in Richfield and Bloomington south of Minneapolis after World War II) led to housing production and consumption behaviors, which yielded chains of housing vacancies, which led eventually to the erosion of business and residential real-estate wealth and years later to housing abandonment in inner-city neighborhoods such as those south of the Minneapolis CBD.

I have shared these models and empirical results in countless undergraduate, graduate, and professional courses, scholarly conferences, public lectures, speeches to city councils, the Metropolitan Council of the Twin Cities, foundation boards and staffs, and consultations with the staffs of housing agencies, legislative committees, and local nonprofit-housing advocates. My former students now work in government and in the private sector in planning, land development, real estate, retailing, and consulting. In recent years, the Metropolitan Council has begun monitoring housing-market activity on a geographic-sector basis—reporting demand, supply and prices, and issuing forecasts for each sector.

Ideas do have impact.

—5—

Uncovering the Complexities of Using Land-Use Planning to Affect Travel Behavior

Kevin J. Krizek

Concerns about traffic congestion, urban sprawl, and urban growth are among the most important issues facing the United States. The Twin Cities are no exception. These concerns now edge out more traditional matters, such as crime and education. In response, public officials, business interests, and citizens aggressively seek strategies to curb automobile reliance and the consequences it engenders (for example, excessively long commutes, seas of parking lots, and increased rates of natural-resource consumption). One would be hard pressed to identify planning efforts in any community in the Twin Cities (Minneapolis and St. Paul metro areas) not striving to make the built environment less auto-reliant and more pedestrian-friendly.

These concerns motivate a powerful new paradigm in urban planning, called "smart growth" in some circles, "new urbanism" or "sustainable development" in others. The strength of this movement hinges in part on the oft-touted relationship between land use and transportation planning. Its main premise is that land-use planning that furthers compact development, a mix of uses, and urban-design improvements (for example, gridded streets, sidewalks, and street crossings) leads to increased walking and spurs transit use. Citizens, political leaders, and land-use and transportation planners locally and nationwide have embraced this development concept, hoping for such benefits. The continuing debate over the existing Hiawatha light-rail line in Minneapolis and extending light rail to other areas is a prime example of such discussions.

But is there sufficient evidence of land-use planning effectively managing the demand for travel? To what degree will land-use policy help community efforts meet the goal of reduced auto use? These issues prompt an interesting research agenda; more importantly, they present important issues to policy officials guarding against unintended or overstated results. Answers will undoubtedly help better position such initiatives against myriad policies competing for support and funding.

Smart-growth advocates claim that members of households living in urban neighborhoods walk more, use transit, and drive less. These assertions may well be the case; they make intuitive sense. Advocates also point to empirical results of studies showing inverse correlations between density and auto use.

As with any aspect of behavioral research, however, such matters are inherently complex. There are important issues—overlooked in most analysis and discussion—related to understanding human behavior, preferences, and the broader societal factors limiting the development of such neighborhoods. Research aiming to shed light on these complex matters has formed the crux of my recent research endeavors. The following describes three matters that inform land-use and transportation-planning initiatives in the metropolitan area of the Twin Cities.

The first issue requires us to better understand basic patterns of travel as they relate to linked trips. Many research efforts separate work trips from nonwork trips and analyze each independently. The theory in doing so is that work trips tend to be more structured, temporally and geographically, while nonwork trips remain more flexible. Bringing nonwork-related land uses closer to people's residences or workplaces, it suggests, will encourage households to shop locally.

But any analysis evaluating trips independently masks the sequential and multipurpose travel of the real world. In my research, I have discovered that, on average, individuals link one or more trips together every other time they leave home. This chaining behavior is important to consider before we make projections about changing how and where people shop.

Consider the following two scenarios. Both Mrs. Smith and Mr. Jones live in a compact neighborhood. Mrs. Smith drives to work and completes several errands (for example, buying groceries or making an appointment) on her way to or from work; each stop is close to her workplace. Despite living close to basic services, her daily travel and shopping preferences prompt choices to shop outside her neighborhood. Mr. Jones drives once a week from home to the dry cleaner. His decision to drive, however, is not because a car is required for his trip to the dry cleaner; he completes the trip to the dry cleaner as part of his weekly trip to the grocer—which itself requires a car.

In each of these cases, the individual's highly compact neighborhood plays a small, if not insignificant, role in driving less. This is because the sequence and combination of trips, not the individual trips themselves, are important considerations. We must examine the larger pattern of linked trips because they work with basic forces that dictate the nature of people's travel. Analyzing a subset of travel behavior—just nonwork trips or just nonlinked trips—helps us to understand an important piece of the puzzle. It is, however, only one piece. And my research shows that this is a piece that, considered independently, may lead to overestimating the effect that land-use policy as proposed by smart-growth proponents has on travel.

A second issue addresses matters of self-selection. Residents many times select residential locations in part to match their travel preferences. For example, some people move to a neighborhood where they can walk to the grocery store because that is an option they prefer. But this suggests that differences in travel between households with different neighborhood design should not be credited to the urban form alone. The differences might be attributable to the broader preferences that trigger the choice to locate in a given neighborhood. An important and troubling issue is that the two effects—urban form and preference—must be disentangled despite the difficulty posed in measuring preferences.

The point is that the relative magnitude of the independent effect of urban form on travel may become marginalized once preferences are accounted for. Put another way, efforts to use urban form to induce unwilling auto-oriented households to drive less may be futile for at least two reasons. First, their auto-using behavior may be a function of larger issues such as their overall preference for auto-oriented behavior. (You can take the family out of the suburbs, but you can't take reliance on the Chevy Suburban out of the family). Second, such auto-oriented households are unlikely to locate in heavily transit-oriented neighborhoods.

This in turn suggests that the success of the smart-growth movement may be limited to the relatively small number of households that currently live in transit-oriented neighborhoods and/or to those who will bring their non-auto-using behavior to any new neighborhood. If there is a self-selection bias at work, policies designed to induce changes in household travel through altering land use may not have the expected or desired effect. Or, at least, their impact may be marginal. Too often, policy officials fail to recognize the role that attitudes and preferences play in influencing travel and location decisions.

A final issue involves the obstacles that must be overcome for such forms of development to come to fruition. They include but are not limited to the difficulty in retrofitting existing development, the questionable demand for such types of neighborhoods, and the ex-urban location of large tracts of developable land. Largely unrecognized, however, are public policies, currently on the books, that impede development based on the ideals of smart growth. Policy officials must not overlook the existing regulatory constraints that shape metropolitan development but run counter to the above-mentioned goals.

Take, for example, zoning that binds upper densities, mandates land-use separation, and limits tracts of development to single-family homes. How about transportation standards calling for wide streets, requiring generous parking requirements, and failing to require sidewalks? Or consider institutional structures that isolate land-use planning decisions from transportation-planning decisions. Some critics have gone so far as to suggest that "urban planners have met the enemy and it is us!"

The urban planning and policy community has put forth templates (for example, a zoning code) that continue to be used as blueprints for shaping auto-reliant urban form. The zoning template impedes progress because the process for obtaining exceptions to the rule is arduous. A community may work to develop a transit-friendly neighborhood, but without a developer willing to wade through the policy molasses involved in seeking variances and the sort, such development rarely comes to fruition. Policy officials often fail to acknowledge how such irony plays out in land-use/transportation initiatives.

As urban planners and policy officials strive to reduce auto-reliant travel, they must strive to understand the myriad issues in doing so. This requires, in part, furthering a dialogue that better explores the reasons for household decisions and the differences between assertions and reality. Advocates, progressive policymakers, and other like-minded individuals are good at furthering an agenda that, in effect, says, "increasing density, furthering pedestrian-friendly design, and building transit will reduce driving." They presume that "smarter" land-use/transportation policy trumps existing behavior, attitudes, and other obstacles. They claim a substantial latent demand for more pedestrian-friendly design. There may be such a demand, but we do not yet know for sure.

My research to date has helped to identify the reasons for approaching this message with caution and even for redirecting the rationales used to further this agenda! The three matters described above—trip chaining, household preferences, and existing land-use/transportation policy—receive little attention in policy discussions. The reality underlying these matters may not cast optimistic light on the potential of the smart-growth movement. But at the same time, such matters do not undermine the other central aims of planning for its pedestrian-friendly urban form.

My primary purpose has been twofold: (1) to draw attention to issues imperative to the understanding of policy officials intending to advance such policies, and (2) to help articulate a sound basis for advancing such efforts. No amount of research is likely to resolve what has now become the proverbial sprawl/smart-growth debate. Many go so far as to suggest that the debate is irresolvable because of the normative, ethical, and moral issues it brings forth.

But that does not mean we should not be uncovering rationales for the advancement of policies. For example, officials may need to motivate smart-growth initiatives less on the merits of reducing congestion and auto-reliant travel and more towards increasing the array of travel and residential choices. In many respects, these very choices may have been constrained in recent years, may even have prevented households from successfully matching land-use and transportation environments to their needs and preferences.

Land-use/transportation policy efforts must focus less on the potential to take cars off the road and more on land-use strategies that increase choice in regard to where people live and how they get around. Doing so may provide clearer justification for such initiatives and less resistance. In the long run, then, we may end up with less congestion.

Part II

Inventing New Techniques
for Managers and Activists

—6—

A Theory of Democratic Governance

Harry C. Boyte

Political education, in the older sense of educating students for complex, boundary-crossing negotiations among diverse groups, has recently emerged as an important theme in public-affairs theory and education. The Center for Democracy and Citizenship at the Humphrey Institute over the two decades of its theory-building partnerships has integrated everyday politics into a range of institutional and community settings. This partnership work, in turn, has generated the conceptual framework of "citizenship as public work," with far-ranging implications for theories of democratic governance, understandings of politics, and the meaning of democracy. Put simply, citizenship as public work points to the citizen as the *cocreator of democracy, understood as a way of life, not simply a set of formal institutions of government.* Public professionals and officeholders, in such a conception, often function more as organizers, catalysts, conveners and educators than as service providers. Government is the resource of citizens and civic institutions, the larger democratic society, neither the savior nor the enemy. And politics is not simply a distributive battle over "who gets what," but a productive activity that solves problems and produces public things. Such a conceptual transformation can be likened to a Copernican revolution, in which citizens, not officials, hold center stage. It also challenges the scarcity mentality that has widely taken hold in our time.

Donald F. Kettl, director of the Fels Institue of Government at the Univeristy of Pennsylvania, set the stage for the importance of public-affairs professionals learning to "think politically" in *The Transformation of Governance: Public Administration for Twenty-First Century America* (2002). He explored the way in which the challenges of public-affairs work in the twenty-first century confound older models of practice based on one-way service delivery and command-and-control structures.

"For a century, the field . . . built its approach on service delivery, basing that service delivery on theories of hierarchy and authority," Kettl wrote.

Dominant theories of policymaking and policy implementation alike reflect such a paradigm. According to Kettl, "Policymakers tend to convey a simple and straightforward view of how the administrative process works—almost like a vending machine, into which they put money and out of which they expect results."

The problem is that the model no longer works in an environment that reflects governance and not simply government. Kettl explained: "In the last decades of the twentieth century . . . more of what government . . . did no longer fit the hierarchical model of authority-driven government . . . Government needed active partnerships with nongovernment partners to accomplish its purposes."

If public-affairs professionals are to realize their potential as civic leaders and catalysts for solving public problems and creating public value, then governance necessitates the retrieval of an older sense of politics, that is, the negotiation of plural interests and the creation of local civic cultures animated by such politics.

Barbara Nelson, dean of UCLA's School of Public Policy and Social Research and formerly a professor at the Humphrey Institute, pointed toward this dynamic in her 2002 address to the National Association of Schools of Public Affairs and Administration (NASPAA). She observed that in complex environments, where conceptions and practices of "the public interest" can never be taken as a given—indeed, must always be negotiated among divergent interests—twenty-first-century public-affairs curricula must "educate students to work successfully at the seams of institutions, sectors, and jurisdictions as well as within them." This means teaching politics. "Perhaps the greatest lack in our curricula has been attention to politics in the Aristotelian sense of the public mediation of conflicts with public consequences, " Nelson has explained.

In 1987, Harlan Cleveland, then dean of the Humphrey Institute, asked me to begin a project aimed at finding workable remedies for democracy's troubles. We sought to translate such politics into a variety of environments, building on resources that had been accumulating in the civic experiments of recent decades at the grassroots of society. This effort became the Center for Democracy and Citizenship (CDC).

In *Civic Innovation in America* (2001) and other works, Carmen Sirianni, professor of sociology and public policy at Brandeis University, and Lewis Friedland, associate professor of journalism and mass communication at the University of Wisconsin, Madison, detailed such civic experiments in community development, health, environmentalism, and other fields.

These efforts bring people of diverse views together to solve public problems and create public wealth. Implicitly or explicitly, such endeavors reconceptualize politics—the authoritative language of public life—as the everyday interactions among citizens of roughly equal standing, in horizontal relationships with each other, not simply in vertical relations with the state.

Such politics are explicitly taught in what is called "broad-based citizen organizing," in groups such as the Industrial Areas Foundation network (IAF), grounded largely in religious congregations of diverse faiths and backgrounds. Building substantial power for ordinary people—the mission of these organizations—involves a molecular organizing process that requires people to learn the disciplines of a philosophically oriented, Aristotelian politics in Nelson's terms—not ideological politics. Such politics draw from theorists such as Bernard Crick, Hannah Arendt, and Sheldon Wolin, against the grain of dominant definitions. Politics is what Crick calls "a civilizing activity," the way that people of diverse interests and views negotiate differences to solve problems and live together without violence.

Such groups have recently gained increasing attention from scholars such as Mark Warren at Harvard, Paul Osterman at MIT, Maribeth Larkin in Texas, and others, for their success in activating large numbers of low-income, minority, and working-class people. They base their philosophical framework on democratic and religious values—justice, participation, human dignity, and open discourse—that can be found across cultural and partisan differences. Such broad-based groups reclaim politics as the free, deprofessionalized, nonpartisan activity of ordinary citizens. They differ from issue organizing by defining their culture as defense of democratic and religious values—the dignity of the person, community relationships, justice and concern for the poor, participation—against the forces of a larger culture that put such values under siege.

A little-observed aspect of their practice is that such politics depends on democratic professional change, the reintegration of professional practices into community life and networks, and the creation of vital local civic cultures. Organizing is reconceived as a profession that focuses on building democratic capacities in communities. Such organizing is framed as different from the "mobilizing" on left and right in which professionals define issues, script the action, and use techniques like the Internet to get people out. In broad-based citizen efforts, organizers are coaches while citizen leaders take center stage. Organizers are mentored and work in networks of support. Citizen ownership of politics, based upon respect for the public potentials of ordinary people, is stressed, What is called the iron rule—never do things for others that they can do for themselves—counters the service-delivery paradigm.

The definition of leader has also shifted in ways that weave citizen action into community life, again in a fashion different from issue mobilization, which often draws activists away. Leaders in community organizing traditionally have been the visible public actors, typically male, who championed causes like ending racial discrimination and police brutality. In broad-based organizing, key leaders are a more invisible tier of community members, frequently women, who work behind the scenes to keep school PTAs going, run day-to-day activities in churches, and the like.

In San Antonio, a Mexican-American group—Communities Organized for Public Service (COPS)—established the pattern for this approach. Organizers call such leaders "community sustainers" or moderates, contrasting them with activists. "COPS built on the basis of PTA leaders, parish council members, stalwarts of the church guilds," said Christine Stephens, lead organizer of COPS during much of this innovation during the 1980s, in my interviews with her. "Not the politicos," she explained, but "the people who have wheeled and dealed."

Stephens sees this as a basic shift in the social basis of citizen action: "This approach builds around the people who have sustained the community, for example, women whose lives by and large have been wrapped up in their parishes and their children." The emphasis creates change in individuals and communities. And, she says, "What COPS has been able to do is to give them a public life, to educate, to provide the tools whereby they can participate in the political process."

Such organizing gives sustained attention to adding public, interactive dimensions to the work of the clergy. Helping members of the clergy to make their work more public is a challenge. "I sometimes say that clergy and cops are alike," Moriba Karamoko, a former IAF organizer, has observed. "I know of no other two professions where the psyche and the persona that come with the profession are so much the same. People carry their work persona with them even to bed. For the average cop, everybody is a suspect. [Members of the] clergy are always in the position of nurturing and giving and counseling and saving. They become fixers."

Karamoko has said that IAF organizing requires members of the clergy to be more relational and reciprocal, to "engage in the public square." Acknowledging that this is often difficult, he explains: "It's not the way they're socialized. The struggle is to help them to envision their role and their life and their contribution being also outside the church. They also have a civic voice. They have issues that are important to them as a pastor, as a voter, as a father, as an uncle, as a god-father." It takes "struggle," he notes, "to get inside their self-interests, their vision, their anger, and their hopes. What do they want to be in a city? How can this work help them?"

Such efforts, involving several networks such as the IAF (Industrial Areas Foundation), Gamaliel Foundation, the Pacific Institute of Community Organizations, and DART, include more than 160 affiliated citizen groups across the country. Yet, for all their successes on practical issues, they can still be dismissed as inspiring but marginal oases of public life in a culture dominated by manipulative media, materialism, radical individualism, and technocratic trends. They succeed in creating relational countercultures, against the grain of a highly individualistic society, and in fighting for a fair share of the pie, in a society tilted toward the rich and powerful. But they have done little to change the culture-making institutions that generate the larger values crisis that they decry.

For nineteen years, the Center for Democracy and Citizenship and its colleagues have theorized and translated such lessons into other contexts, based on the premise that everyday politics holds large implications for renewing and strengthening democratic governance and changing a culture increasingly driven by materialism, the cult of efficiency, and winning at any price. In the practice and theory of the Center for Democracy and Citizenship and its colleagues, creating democratic governance involves three elements:

1. Everyday Politics: Translation of the methods of citizen organizing elsewhere by naming its practices and ideas as a politics that can be practiced generally

2. Citizen Professionals: The democratization of professional practices to shift from service delivery to public work grounded in local civic life, with careful attention to the methods and contexts in which democratic professional craft can be learned and the ways in which democratic professional practice can renew civic cultures

3. Renewal of the Commonwealth: A shift in paradigm meanings of democracy, from democratic state to democracy as a way of life or a society, with shared civic responsibility for the generation of public goods and a culture-changing emphasis that points beyond scarcity toward the multiple untapped resources for problem solving.

The Center for Democracy and Citizenship and its colleagues have developed initiatives that show the possibilities for spreading such politics in varied settings. In Public Achievement, for instance, teams of young people, ranging from elementary through high-school students, work over months on a public issue they choose. Adult coaches help them to develop achievable goals and learn political skills and concepts. The teams address a range of issues, including teen pregnancy, racism, violence, and curriculum.

Sometimes, young people achieve remarkable results. For instance, at St. Bernard's Elementary School in St. Paul, the incubator school of Public Achievement in the 1990s, teams of students in the sixth and seventh grades worked on one issue—building a playground in a low-income area.

To succeed, the teams had to turn neighborhood opinion around on the playground issue (neighbors had originally thought that a playground might be a magnet for gangs). They had to get the parish council on their side, negotiate zoning changes with city officials, and raise $60,000 from local businesses.

To accomplish these feats, the children had to learn how to hold each other accountable, chair meetings, interview people, write letters, give speeches, and call people they didn't know on the telephone.

They came to understand the views of adults they once thought were mean and oppressive, to negotiate, make alliances, raise money, map power, and do research. Young people in the effort also learned about political concepts—power, civic engagement and citizenship, public life, diverse interests, and politics.

The Public Achievement framework stresses this sort of effort as everyday politics of public problem-solving and creation. In Public Achievement, young people are conceived as citizens today, not simply as citizens in preparation. They are cocreators of the democratic way of life in their schools, neighborhoods, and society.

In 2004–05 about three thousand young people participated in Public Achievement at more than eighty sites in a number of American communities (the Twin Cities and suburbs; Mankato, Minnesota; Kansas City, Missouri; Kansas City, Kansas; northwestern Missouri; Milwaukee; Denver, Boulder, and Fort Collins, Colorado; Manchester, New Hampshire; Broward County, Florida; and at new sites in San Francisco). Public Achievement has also spread to Northern Ireland, Turkey, Palestine, Israel, Poland, Romania, Moldova, Bosnia, Scotland, Ghana, and South Africa.

Joe Kunkel, a political scientist at the State University of Minnesota/Mankato, whose students coach in a local school, sees an awakening of political interest among young people from small-town and rural areas. "I am amazed by what I have learned," said one. "Not only did I learn to be an effective coach, I also learned about what it means to be an active citizen. We coaches are in a sense renewing democracy for future generations. It has become clear to me through this course that the concept of democracy in America has lost much of its luster and it must be restored" (*Mankato Public Achievement,* 2004). Public-affairs graduate students at the Humphrey Institute who coach in Public Achievement report a similar broadening of their ideas of politics and democracy.

Public Achievement has also been translated into other settings in ways that suggest the possibility of democratic governance in many venues. For instance, the Urban Teacher Program of Minneapolis Community and Technical College has integrated Public Achievement into its curriculum, combining its focus on public skills with preparing students to engage the urban environments where they will work.

Colgate University, a liberal arts school in Hamilton, New York, has integrated everyday politics of public work into its student-affairs and student-life programming. "Our students lacked the basic skills needed to do the work of democracy," Adam Weinberg, dean of the college, explained. These include, in part, public speaking, active listening, conflict resolution, negotiation, and organizing. To teach such skills, students needed a much more robust definition of democracy, citizenship, and politics.

"We wanted students to understand democracy as something they were responsible for producing," said Weinberg. Colgate developed a

comprehensive civic-education effort built around ideas of civic engagement as the everyday politics of public work and democracy as a
society, not simply elections.

To effect this agenda has required a self-conscious challenge to
the service paradigm that has taken hold in student affairs. Weinberg
argues: "Living in a democracy [means] learning to live and work with
people you may not like. We remind students that the roommate who
is 'driving them crazy' will someday be their neighbor, family member,
coworker, or ally on a local issue." Colgate changed residential advisors
from service providers to "democracy coaches," working with students
to address everyday problems.

Public Achievement's growth points toward a second key element
in democratic governance: Teaching everyday politics can democra-
tize professional practices and reground them in local civic cultures.
Strengthening civic practices of officeholders, civil servants, and other professionals entails a paradigm shift from professionals as service
providers to partners, organizers, educators, and catalysts for citizen
action.

The Center for Democracy and Citizenship and its colleagues have
also translated lessons from citizen organizing into professional work
that stresses partnership over service delivery. This emphasis emerged
from the initial premise that the cultures of institutions and communities—not simply individual proclivities, values, or skills—are enormously important in civic engagement. The civic life and cultures of
communities can be conceived as free spaces in which people act on
concrete interests, receive tangible benefits, and develop civic identi-
ties. In free spaces people learn skills of dealing with others—negotiation and problem solving, the messy improvisations of public life.
They also learn to see themselves as responsible agents and architects
of the democracy.

These skills, habits, and values once existed in abundance in the
Upper Midwest. Unions, for instance, were often intricately involved

in the life of their communities. The black Minnesota union leader Nellie Stone Johnson recalled that into the 1950s unions had storefront offices, where people socialized, discussed issues, and undertook community projects.

Free spaces with roots in everyday life connected people with the larger public world and contributed greatly to local civic life. Thus, the late Vice President Hubert H. Humphrey traced his political career to his father's drug store in Doland, South Dakota. It was a public space for talk and action, as well as a civic center of the community.

"In his store there was eager talk about politics, town affairs, and religion," Humphrey wrote. "I've listened to some of the great parliamentary debates of our time but have seldom heard better discussions of basic issues than I did as a boy, standing on a wooden platform behind the soda fountain."

The store was a lending library. Music floated from the window. "[As] a druggist in a tiny town in the middle of the continent, American history and world affairs were as real to him as they were in Washington," wrote Humphrey. "Time after time, when he read about some political development . . . he'd say, 'You should know this, Hubert. It might affect your life someday.'"

The drug store functioned as a free public space because his father was a citizen pharmacist and citizen businessman of Doland. The chapter title in Humphrey's book makes the point: "Never a Pill without an Idea." His father worked in public ways. He championed public goods. He educated public citizens and learned from them as well.

The concept of democracy as society (not simply as elections), had wide appeal. It conveyed the robust civic agency that Alexis de Tocqueville observed in his travels in the 1830s. He noted that Americans typically addressed problems (that in Europe would be handed over to officials) through cooperative action.

In the twentieth century, intellectuals as diverse as Jane Addams, John Dewey, and James Weldon Johnson saw democracy as "a way of life" (Dewey's phrase) far beyond mere elections. Local civic institutions often had parochial elements. Yet they also created civic muscle and were sometimes seedbeds for broad movements such as the New Deal and, later, the civil-rights movement.

In recent decades, as Tom Bender, William Sullivan, Ellen Langeman and others have documented, professionals across fields have come to understand themselves as disciplinary specialists delivering services and detached from the civic culture of places, not as citizens working in horizontal relationships with other citizens.

Those involved in civic-engagement experiments at the Humphrey Institute saw the potential for regenerating civic professionalism and renewed local civic cultures through work in the early 1990s with cooperative extension, the nationwide system of county agents (agriculture, 4-H, home economics, and others) coordinated by land-grant universities.

Scott Peters, a graduate-student researcher with the Center for Democracy and Citizenship, discovered a rich but largely forgotten civic history of the extension service before World War II that stressed agents as organizers and partners, not as expert service providers. Adding strong civic dimensions to their specific expertise, extension workers collaborated with communities to build capacities for cooperative public work that solved problems and broadly aimed to build thriving rural democracy.

Many in cooperative extension showed interest in reviving this tradition. In Anniston, Alabama, for instance, Barbara Mobley, a county cooperative-extension county agent for twenty-nine years, changed to an everyday politics approach. Instead of providing information and services, she helped people organize their own problem-solving groups. This meant "letting go of previous methods we used in prescribing a 'fix' for a community problem," Mobley explained. "We shared the ownership and redefined our role to be a catalyst."

As a result, people began using extension resources in new ways.

An area-wide health council brought together public-health nurses, low-income mothers, and teenagers to tackle problems like teen pregnancy. A group called the Women's Empowerment Network provided training in political skills and public speaking for low-income women. Cooperative extension also organized public meetings of community residents and military personnel to develop a strategic plan for decommissioning chemical weapons.

Similar patterns of democratic professional practice with implications for governance have developed out of partnership work with new immigrants, nursing homes, family medical practices, schools, and institutions of higher education.

The Jane Addams School for Democracy, a learning and public-work partnership on the West Side of St. Paul of Hmong, Latino, and East African communities with area colleges and universities, stresses that all participants are "members." For students, for instance, this shifts from the idea of doing service to collaborative learning.

Generally, this approach has generated democratization of professional practice. Jane Addams School has spawned a neighborhood initiative in which the whole community and its institutions—from parents to libraries, businesses, community organizations, and non-profits—have claimed authority for the education of children. Many new forms of collaboration have emerged. For instance, in the summer of 2004, seventeen youth and community organizations collaborated to design, fund, and coordinate a nine-week, summer daycamp. Neighborhood residents and parents were among the teachers hired. The camp stressed community locations, topics, and resources. The West Side's Educators' Institute helps teachers to discover educational resources of community life.

Other partnerships have suggested possibilities for developing democratic professional practice on a large scale. For instance, William Doherty, a professor of family social science, and his colleagues, have learned to function as democratic organizers with families on issues like overscheduling, media violence, the pressures of consumerism, and other destructive cultural trends. They show how professionals can contribute to citizens reclaiming civic authority and developing power to address the sometimes inchoate but profound discontents of middle-class life and the toxic effects of a culture that sentimentalizes families but in many ways undermines them.

Their partnerships, Families and Democracy, have discovered that developing democratic professional practice requires careful mentoring. It is not mainly "book learned." It involves the skills of listening, understanding community life, developing political talents, and, most subtly, of professionals developing a new, deeper civic identity themselves. It also involves making explicit the tacit political and civic skills of those already engaged in public professional work.

The partnerships have also begun to generate seedbeds for civic agency, with large political and democratic potential. For instance, the community-based parent-education initiative undertaken with the parent-educators' network in Minnesota, which each year involves more than 250,000 parents of young children in parent-education classes, has developed an approach that makes parent educators into coaches for civic action, both individual and collective, on issues that parents identify. Its mission is to develop the capacities of parents for deliberation and public work on issues related to their children's well-being.

Parent educators and parents have found that every issue of parenting—from toilet training to bedtimes and aggressive behaviors—has public dimensions that can be acted upon by individuals and groups. Focus-group research connected to the initiative has also surfaced hidden discontents in suburban communities on issues like family over-scheduling and media violence that may prompt citizen work.

Melissa Stone, a professor at the Humphrey Institute, has asked trenchant questions about governance dynamics that root policy in network structures with diffuse authority: "How must we conceptualize accountability when the actual implementers of public policy are removed from government agencies and have their own notions of to whom and for what they are accountable?" Put differently, what is to prevent corporations, nonprofits, and others from advancing their own interests at the expense of the public good? If public-affairs scholars and practitioners are to realize the possibilities for civic leadership, a theory of democratic governance must engage questions of the meaning of democracy.

If no easily identifiable group of people is to be held to singular account for producing outcomes of broad public benefit, then an ethos of public responsibility, accountability, and authority must become diffused, must become a function of the general civic culture. Governance intimates a paradigm shift both in civic agency—who is to address public problems and promote the general welfare—and in the meaning of democracy. It highlights the productive, community building, public-wealth-generating sides of politics.

This shift can be illustrated by the public-work theory of common-pool resources. Recently, governance theorists have challenged the rational-choice model of public goods, or common-pool resources, developed by Garrett Hardin in his classic 1968 piece, "Tragedy of the Commons" (*Science* 162).

In her pioneering work *Governing the Commons: The Evolution of Institutions for Collective Action* (1990), Elinor Ostrom examined the question of governance, what she terms "the search for rules to improve the efficiency, sustainability, and equity of outcomes," in common-pool settings. She looked at cases of forest management, irrigation, inshore fishery, and the Internet. In each case, she agreed with Hardin that the problem is "excluding free riders," or those who use a commons resource with no regard for its sustainability.

But Ostrom found that decentralized governance with higher popular participation has key advantages in terms of efficiency, sustainability, and equity. These include incorporation of local knowledge, greater involvement of those who are trustworthy and respect principles of reciprocity, feedback on subtle changes in the resource, better adapted rules, lower enforcement costs, and redundancy, which decreases the likelihood of a systemwide failure. Decentralized systems also have disadvantages, such as uneven involvement by local users, the possibilities for "local tyrannies" and discrimination, lack of innovation and access to scientific knowledge, and inability to cope with large common-pool resources.

Ostrom argued persuasively for a mix of decentralized and general governance, what she calls "polycentric governance systems . . . where citizens are able to organize not just one but multiple governing authorities at different scales." Such mixed systems may be messy, but in studies of local economies, "messy polycentric systems significantly outperformed metropolitan areas served by a limited number of large-scale, unified governments."

A public-work perspective adds to governance perspectives in public-goods theory. It emphasizes the civic learning and sense of ownership that develop through commons-building labors by groups of people. Most dramatically in a political culture that takes public wealth for granted even as it privatizes public goods of all kinds, public work draws attention to the *creation* of public goods, the *what* that is generated, as well as the *how* and *to whom* it is distributed through politics.

One example of commons-creation theory informed by the public-work framework is the scholarship of Peter Levine, Institute for Philosophy and Public Policy, University of Maryland, on Internet technology grounded in local commons created and sustained by citizens and civic associations. Levine, building on work that the CDC did with the political campaigns of Al Gore and John McCain in 2000, has highlighted the heritage of "associational commons," or commons managed and sustained by groups of citizens (*The Good Society*, 2003).

In treating the emergence and survival of the Internet as a commons, an associational, community-based, public-work approach has several advantages over anarchist notions. These include the potential political clout, civic learning, and stakeholding that a sense of ownership through shared work can bring. Such an approach also draws specific attention to how public goods come into existence. From the anarchist perspective, the Internet simply appeared as the result of millions of anonymous users. A public-work lens illuminates the complex, detailed labors on the part of government and higher education, researchers, entrepreneurs, and designers responsible for the creation of this commons. This approach also highlights the important role of public institutions such as libraries in the new information commons, a role highlighted recently by the American Library Association and the Free Expression Project of the New York University School of Law (see http://www.fepproject.org).

Public work, when framed as the large task of creating democratic communities and a democratic society, generates an ethos of broad civic accountability, authority, and responsibility. It challenges the consumerist, distributive, rights-based politics that demands more from government, on left or right, but that feeds a political culture in which winning at any cost and material acquisition are often seen as the most important goals.

The idea of democracy as a society created through public work denies neither the crucial importance of elections nor the necessity of government's providing leadership, resources, tools, and rules, nor the importance of struggles for distributive justice. Yet officials are not the center of the civic universe. That role belongs to citizens. And material goods are not the highest mark of a good society—civic life rests in more fundamental ways on the quality of relationships, the cultures and institutions of learning and knowledge generation, the cultivation of beauty, the extent to which an ethos of the common good is widely shared. Democratic society recalls President Jimmy Carter's argument in his farewell address that the only office in a democracy greater than that of president is that of citizen. In a democratic society, government is *of* the people and *by* the people—it is not only *for* them. It is also not the only site of public problem-solving and public-value creation. Government is the resource of free, self-reliant citizens.

Figure Out What They Want,
How to Get It, and Why

John M. Bryson

Over the past twenty-eight years the Humphrey Institute has been a place where I—working with my colleagues—have been able to improve my skill in helping others to determine what they want, how to get it, and why. That skill has taken many forms, including work in the areas of group-process design and facilitation, project planning and management, strategic planning and management, leadership, and organizational design. Each of these areas, but especially strategic planning and management, continually present challenging intellectual puzzles.

During a sabbatical year in 1986–87, I wrote the first edition of a book called *Strategic Planning for Public and Nonprofit Organizations* (San Francisco: Jossey-Bass, 1988, 1995, 2004). The book, now in its third edition, has sold more than a hundred thousand copies and thus is one of the best-selling planning books of all time. Strategic planning is there described as "a disciplined effort to produce fundamental decisions and actions that shape and guide what an organization (or other entity) is, what it does, and why it does it." This definition implies that the purpose of strategic planning is not to create a strategic plan, although formal plans may be helpful, but to affirm or alter an organization's mission, identity, strategies, and justification.

This definition also emphasizes the importance of linking strategic planning and implementation to create what is now called strategic management. The book and the accompanying workbook, *Creating and Implementing Your Strategic Plan* (San Francisco: Jossey-Bass, 1996, 2004), coauthored with Farnum Alston, provide a conceptual and theoretical overview of strategic planning and management along with step-by-step guidance through the process. The ideas in the book and workbook ultimately have touched thousands of organizations and millions of people around the globe.

When I first began working on strategic planning, there were many skeptics. They said strategic planning did not work, never would, and was a waste of time. The late and famous Prof. Aaron Wildavsky comes to mind. So does the former head of the British Civil Service College, who told me in 1986, while I was writing the first edition: "There is no need for strategic planning in the British Civil Service." Within two years I was teaching dozens of civil servants, including the most senior, how to do strategic planning. Where? At the Civil Service College!

In the United States, recent surveys indicate that virtually all nonprofit organizations say they do strategic planning; the vast majority of municipalities and state agencies also say they do. All federal agencies are required to prepare strategic plans.

Where did my work begin? A life's work often has something to do with a person's early experience, and that is certainly true for me. I grew up in what is now euphemistically called a dysfunctional family. Determining what was best for me and those I loved was a serious challenge. Experience as a student in the tumultuous 1960s and as a

VISTA volunteer in Georgia in the early 1970s helped redirect my efforts toward broader and more important public purposes. Along the way I made a profoundly important discovery: It is not enough simply to have good ideas for another's situation. One must help people to come up with their own good ideas, around which they can organize a winning coalition. The quest to develop concepts, procedures, and tools that help others come to know what they want, why they want it, and how to get it became my calling.

I did not invent strategic planning. Indeed, many of the ideas that are at the heart of strategic planning have ancient origins. Even the word *strategy* comes from two Greek words, *stratus* or army and *ego* or leader. Strategic planning started out as the art of the general and has become the art of the general manager. The Chinese philosopher Sun Tzu 2,500 years ago essentially invented the SWOT analysis—for strengths, weaknesses, opportunities, and threats—a standard strategic planning tool. In the twentieth century, most of the work on strategic planning was done in and for the business sector. Others and I built on and adapted that work to public and nonprofit purposes. My particular contributions to the field are:

- making strategic planning intelligible and operational to reflective practitioners in public and nonprofit organizations
- creating an easily understandable model of strategic planning and management, called the Strategy Change Cycle, that includes all of the important planning and implementation steps and is clearly tied to the relevant public, business, and nonprofit literatures
- encouraging people to pay attention to the "initial agreement" phase of strategic planning, when the basics of the process and necessary early commitments are worked out

- emphasizing the importance of attending to stakeholders—those who are involved in or affected by the process—and providing a set of tools for analyzing stakeholders and their interests
- providing people with other easy-to-use tools for accomplishing important tasks throughout the process
- identifying and highlighting the leadership tasks that must be accomplished for a strategic planning process to succeed.

Many people have contributed to this work. While I was an assistant professor, Harlan Cleveland, the first dean of the Humphrey Institute, helped fund a project that I directed on the nature of leadership, planning, and management in "shared-power" environments. The language of shared power was unusual and provocative in the early 1980s. Now it is taken for granted by most savvy public and nonprofit professionals that we live and work in a shared-power world. One strand of the work resulted in a prize-winning book on leadership written with Barbara Crosby called *Leadership for the Common Good* (San Francisco: Jossey-Bass, 1992, 2005), now in its second edition. The other strand resulted in my books, chapters, and articles on strategic planning.

In 1984, former Humphrey Institute professor Robert C. Einsweiler and I organized an international conference—"Shared Power: What Is It? How Does It Work? How Can We Make It Work Better?" One participant was Prof. Bernard Taylor of Henley Management College in England. As he and I drove on westbound I-94 over Cedar Avenue in Minneapolis, he said, "You know, John, there is not a good book on public-sector strategic planning. You should write it!" I spent my sabbatical leave two years later doing just that.

I could not have written that first book on strategic planning without the help, advice, and guidance of Robert Einsweiler. As a result of Taylor's prompting, Einsweiler and I co-taught a course on strategic planning at the institute that was extraordinarily useful preparation. Einsweiler is the best public-sector strategist I have ever known. Teaching a case-based course together educated me as much as it did the students.

In addition, I am deeply grateful for the contributions and friendship over the years of Profs. Colin Eden and Fran Ackermann of the University of Strathclyde in Scotland, and of former Humphrey colleague Charles Finn, now on the faculty of the College of St. Rose in Albany, New York. There are many others—too many to name them all—without whose encouragement, advice, contributions, friendship, and frequent criticism my work would have had much less impact.

In 2002–03 I devoted a sabbatical year to writing the now-published third edition of the strategic-planning book. This edition includes even more attention to initial agreements and stakeholder analyses, and to leadership, collaboration, performance management, and other topics.

The real challenge in the third edition was to confront and figure out how to address the three major trends in contemporary strategic planning and management. The three trends are a need for:

1. increased inclusiveness, in which more different kinds of people and different kinds of expertise are included
2. enhanced "systems thinking," in which various kinds of analytic methods and tools are employed to help understand the system being planned for and managed, and to help design effective strategies
3. increased speed of the process.

In my experience, one can address any two of the trends without too much difficulty. The challenge lies in addressing all three simultaneously. Discerning what to say about handling these challenges is precisely the kind of intellectual puzzle that has enthralled me for decades. I can't say that I am fully satisfied with what I was able to say in the third edition, but there is always the prospect of a fourth!

—8—

Rethinking Leadership

Robert Terry & Barbara Crosby

America's fate and direction depend on citizen leaders in every nook and cranny of our great nation. Remember that leaders come in both genders, all sizes, ages, from all geographic areas and neighborhoods.

—Marian Wright Edelman

The salvation of the world lies nowhere else than in the human heart, in the human power to reflect, in human modesty, and in human responsibility.

—Vaclav Havel, *Art of the Impossible*

I went into the Reflective Leadership year as one person, and when I came out, I was profoundly different.

—Debra Frasier, author/artist

In the early days of the Humphrey Institute's Reflective Leadership Center, we confronted a vexing challenge: how to teach a subject—leadership—that was ill-defined yet deemed crucial to improving the practice of public affairs. Among academics and practitioners we found an amazing array of ideas about what leadership is and about what goes into effective leadership. Everyone seemed to agree that leadership was important, but that was about all.

As we sought readings for our leadership seminars in the early 1980s, we found numerous studies and biographies of top positional leaders in business and government but little consideration of leaders other than CEOs and presidents. Those identified as leaders tended to be "white" American men. Meanwhile, we intentionally included women, people of color, and people from other countries in our seminar recruitment efforts. We were caught in the dilemma of teaching a subject full of conflicting views and massive gaps.

So we decided to teach leadership while trying to figure out what it was, a process akin to building a bridge as you cross it. We organized a think tank of scholars and practitioners who met frequently at the center's original home at 2610 University Avenue in Minneapolis, to argue about definitions of leadership and to identify sound leadership theory and analysis. We invited insightful leadership scholars such as James MacGregor Burns, Barbara Kellerman, Harold Prince, and Ronald Heifetz to meet with our seminars and with the think tank. From these conversations eventually emerged frameworks that became known as the Diamond Model, the Leadership Action Wheel, and Leadership for the Common Good.

These leadership-framing tools allowed us to sort the variety of leadership perspectives into different schools of thought, highlight the connections among them, and point out in each the most supportable insights and most glaring areas of neglect. Perhaps most importantly, these tools helped people in our seminars apply leadership research to their own leadership challenges and supported our effort to highlight leadership among all groups of people, at all levels of organizations, and in all societies. The frame behind our frameworks was what we saw as the seven main dimensions of human action—existence, resources, structure, power, mission, meaning, and fulfillment.

By clustering schools of leadership and linking them to dimensions of action, we pioneered a breakthrough to diagnosis. For the first time in the field of leadership studies, there was a way to frame what was going on in organizations and communities and to match that to appropriate leadership actions.

Most previous scholarship had focused on leadership connected to resource and structure dimensions—that is, team and organizational leadership. We argued for more attention to the other dimensions. Thus we joined the then-small but now-flourishing group of scholars who attend to the connection of leadership to power, vision, ethics, and spirituality.

Our research led to the publication of *Leadership for the Common Good* (John M. Bryson and Barbara C. Crosby, San Francisco: Jossey-Bass, 1992, now in its second edition) and *Authentic Leadership* (Robert Terry, San Francisco: Jossey-Bass, 1993). The first of these focuses on leadership for policy change and connects different types of leadership to different phases of the policy-change cycle. The second explicates the Leadership Action Wheel and highlights the courage needed to bring authenticity to personal, organizational, and community life.

Diverse Programs and Audiences

During the first decade, the Center for Reflective Leadership's programming proliferated. We continued to offer the signature nine-month Leadership in Public Policy seminar, which attracted midcareer learners from government, nonprofit organizations, business, organized labor, the arts, and education. We organized leadership programs for the Humphrey Institute's international fellows, for arts educators from

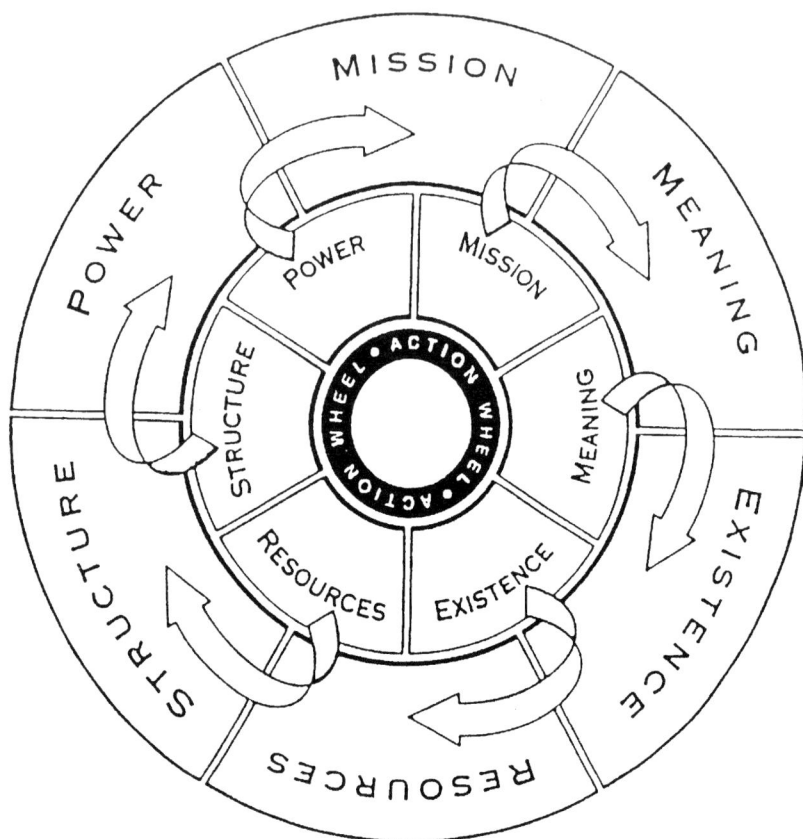

The Leadership Action Wheel

around the country, for school superintendents, for state legislators and legislative staff, for the City of St. Paul, and for clergy, among others. In partnership with the Junior League, we started a groundbreaking Women in Leadership program. At one point we collaborated with artist Suzanne Lacy on an innovative Leadership for Older Women program that culminated in a participatory performance in the atrium of a downtown Minneapolis skyscraper. We supported Nora Hall, an alumna of our signature seminar, in creating a Leadership for Black Women program.

In the mid-1980s, Gerry Miller, an administrator in agricultural extension at the University of Minnesota, asked the Reflective Leadership Center to cocreate a four-year program for extension educators. Named LEAD (Leadership Education And Development), it included sessions at locations in Minnesota, a visit to Washington, D.C., and a trip to Europe. Prof. Donna Rae Scheffert worked with us to create and make LEAD one of the center's most successful programs. Later, we expanded the program to focus on rural leaders in Iowa and Minnesota and named that iteration M/I LEAD (Minnesota/Iowa Leadership Education And Development). Participants in LEAD and M/ILEAD report that these programs continue to shape their leadership.

In addition to these extended-period programs, we provided leadership workshops or consultations for nonprofit or governmental organizations, mainly in the United States. We convened an All-University Leadership Council to bring scholars from various fields together to share research findings and teaching methodologies.

During most of the center's second decade, Sharon Anderson and then Prof. John Bryson served as its director. More books, fieldbooks, and articles flowed from the Reflective Leadership group. In 1999, we launched a project, called Organizing Hope, in partnership with the University of Minnesota Extension Service. It included a website and an on-line tutorial. Also, in 1999, the Leadership for Common Good seminar (successor to Leadership in Public Policy) became a core course in a new midcareer master's degree program offered both at the Humphrey Institute and at the University of Warmia and Mazury in Poland. The center also was a key partner in launching the University of Minnesota's leadership minor, which graduated its first class in 2000.

Making a Difference

Two decades after the center began, we have considerable evidence of the impact of our programs and publications on the life journey of individual learners, on organizations (including the University of Minnesota), on communities, and on the field of leadership studies.

Individual Impacts

Extensive evaluations of our seminars and workshops indicate that the programs helped participants understand leadership theories and tools, develop useful strategies for their leadership work, claim their leadership potential, and build learning communities. Participants expressed appreciation for the opportunity to acquire a larger view, or systems understanding. They said that before participating in our programs they had been able to see pieces of systems but not how they were connected. Recently we asked alumni of our programs to tell stories describing the long-term impacts of the programs. These stories reveal two main themes:

1. Participants gained from the programs a heightened sense of their leadership potential and responsibility.
2. They developed the courage to undertake new initiatives, ranging from an antiracism campaign to a women's leadership program.

Following are sample comments from the alumni stories: Arvonne Fraser, senior fellow emerita, wrote, "Participating in that seminar gave me the courage to develop a project at the Humphrey Institute dealing with women internationally. It also contributed to my starting the Center on Women and Public Policy at the institute and codirecting it with Prof. Barbara Nelson."

Debra Frasier, author and artist, said, "I went into the Reflective Leadership year as one person, and when I came out, I was profoundly different . . . I now look at the world from a ridge instead of a valley. I live and work in the valley, but I have this ridge that I can go to at any moment, and from this ridge I can see further into a more inclusive view . . . Once I called the gifts from Reflective Leadership a kind of 'time release magic' . . . The people and the information do continue to unfold throughout time, and the result is a kind of magic—the ability to transform."

Marcia Casey Cushmore, consultant and artist, wrote: "I learned that the single greatest step toward solving the challenges and problems I was brought in to work on was for an individual or a group of individuals to 'get their own lives in order.' Living our own lives well is the greatest leadership challenge and opportunity any of us will ever have. And incidentally, it is the most powerful thing on earth."

Scott Jensen is a physician whose participation in the Leadership for the Common Good seminar prompted him to run again for a school board seat. He won and was soon embroiled in wrenching controversy but concluded that the involvement was worth the grief. He asked would-be leaders: "What will it be—go along, get along, and find approval? Or will it be—take a stand, make a mark, seek not popularity or celebration, but rather make the choice to unflinchingly commit to doing one's best and leaving it at that?"

Dick Little, planner and community activist, wrote: "The leadership year (1989–90) led to some radical changes in my priorities, focus of energy, and use of time. I embarked on a very different journey, in which my major activities have been dictated by a leadership vision and tools I developed at the Humphrey Institute, including 1) connecting my personal and public policy passions, 2) focusing on 'making a difference,' 3) learning to lead from my strengths, 4) valuing ethical and spiritual leadership as equal to or greater than positional leadership, and 5) taking on issues that aren't being dealt with by society . . . In the course of this journey, I have been propelled into some leadership 'callings' and leadership initiatives, focusing on some of the most significant ethical, moral, and political challenges of our time—racism, segregation, and equality of opportunity. A change of job, career, and vocation also occurred as part of this journey . . . Based on my convictions, I left a good job [with HUD] with a comfortable salary and benefits package to pursue an unknown path of civic/voluntary leadership and service contributions . . . a decision that made headlines in the American Planning Association's *Planning* magazine."

Impact on the University of Minnesota

The All-University Leadership Council and its successor the Leadership and Change Affinity group greatly increased cooperation among faculty and student affairs staff interested in leadership. This cooperation led to new or richer leadership courses and programs around the Twin Cities campus. Perhaps the most outstanding legacy of the affinity group is the university's new leadership minor. The Reflective Leadership Center also helped the University of Minnesota Extension Service build programming and expertise in community and political leadership. It started with LEAD and M/ILEAD and extended through ongoing work with Extension's community vitality programs. The center's midcareer leadership seminars laid groundwork for the Humphrey Institute's midcareer Master of Public Affairs degree, which graduated its first class in 1999.

Impact on Leadership Studies

We are among a group of leadership scholars who have prompted a sea change in the field of leadership studies (and in so doing helped define the field) over the last dozen years. The group's publications and other professional activities have given new prominence to the effects of gender and culture on leadership, to the leader-follower relationship, to nonpositional leadership, and to the connections of leadership, ethics, and spirituality.

We also have contributed to learning about leadership teaching. Through extensive evaluation of our courses and workshops and continual revision of our methods, we discovered what helps midcareer adults from around the world improve their leadership practice. (We've also found that the same general approach, with modification, works with many other audiences.) Our experience jibes with what several other leadership educators have reported in recent years. We have identified several hallmarks of successful leadership development programs:

- a focus on assessing and strengthening individual leadership capacity
- exercises and cases linked to learners' developmental tasks
- assessment and strengthening of collective leadership capacity
- attention to participants' real work—that is, their professional issues and problems
- extended learning periods—programs that last for several months and have continuing opportunities for networking have greater impact.

Leadership educators also have a growing interest in the use of reflection in leadership education, an approach pioneered by the center. In November 2001, one of us led a session on "Reflective Leadership Education" at the International Leadership Association's annual conference. What was planned as a small roundtable discussion became a sprawling, energetic conversation as people jammed the room to find out how others were using reflection in leadership courses and workshops. The turnout and lively discussion demonstrated that the brand of leadership education developed by the Reflective Leadership Center over the last twenty years continues to attract interest and energy.

In 2004, the Reflective Leadership Center became a part of the Humphrey Institute's new Public and Nonprofit Leadership Center.

—9—

The Peace Dividend:
Moving Resources from Defense
to Development

Ann Markusen

If there is one "new century" trend giving us hope in the world and at home, it is conflict resolution and its companions—cooperation, education, and investment—in place of war, destruction, and privatization. The 1990s comprised a period of remarkable progress in peaceful transition from South Africa and the former Soviet Union to, somewhat more tentatively, Northern Ireland and the Middle East. Spending on the military plummeted almost 40 percent worldwide.

Although tensions and a worrisome rise in militarism still percolate, our knowledge and practice of conflict resolution have expanded enormously. Almost everyone, even our military leaders, would agree that investments such as clean water, agricultural productivity, and above all, education, are far more powerful in achieving human welfare than spending on war and defense. The billions being spent on the current war with Iraq have not appreciably stimulated the domestic economy, but they have cut into investments in education, health care, and infrastructure.

For more than a decade, I worked with economists, planning colleagues, and graduate students to analyze the military-civilian divide and formulate policy responses for moving resources to the civilian sector in post-conflict periods. I owe special thanks to economist Michael Oden for joining my project as a postdoctoral fellow and playing a major role in this effort.

In *The Rise of the Gunbelt* (Markusen, Hall, Campbell, and Deitrick, 1991), my colleagues and I examined how the United States bred entire regional economies—in San Diego, Los Alamos, Colorado Springs, and Huntsville, Alabama, for example—around the activities of war. In *Dismantling the Cold War Economy* (Markusen and Yudken, 1992), Joel Yudken and I laid out a program for moving defense-dependent industries, companies, workers, technologies, and communities into productive, economy-building uses. In *Arming the Future* (Markusen and Costigan, 1999), Sean Costigan and I took on the defense industry and addressed the influences—corporate greed, Wall Street, soft corruption in politics, and lax public vigilance—undermining the gains of the 1990s. In *America's Peace Dividend* (Markusen, ed., 2000), I laid out a program for the twenty-first century, arguing for restraint in military buildup.

In *From Defense to Development* (Markusen, DiGiovanna, and Leary, 2003), Sean DiGiovanna, Michael Leary, and I tackled the problem of how to reorient economic resources released by the end of military conflicts towards wealth-creating and poverty-alleviating investments and productive activity in many countries of the world. And we extended the analysis to heavily military-invested countries around the world—India, South Korea, China, South Africa, Israel, Argentina, Poland, Russia, Spain, Germany, and France—assessing how they took advantage of the end of the Cold War and regional hostilities to reorient resources towards peaceable economic activities.

Why did the project of defense conversion require an intellectual agenda and a research component? Free marketers, such as Murray Weidenbaum (1992), argued that private decision-makers would reallocate the resources with no problem and that government should not intervene. Defense-conversion advocates such as Seymour Melman (1970, 1974, 1983, 1988), whose powerful moral and economic arguments for conversion inspired many activists, underestimated the institutional and industrial blockages that made difficult the moving of men and machines from fashioning swords to plowshares on the same shop floor. The goal of our team of collaborators was to provide a nuanced, politically sophisticated, and empirically tested account of how defense conversion could and should proceed. The final stages of this work have taken place at the Humphrey Institute and were nourished by the resources there.

Our research effort has been action- and policy-oriented from its inception. Our action agenda stretched from the local level, where we chose partners with large stakes in defense conversion, to the national and even international levels, working at all scales with many protagonists—peace activists, labor unions, economic development organizations, industry associations, small businesses, mayors in military-base and defense-plant communities, and government and military officials responsible for the defense build-down. We grounded our work in sound economic and moral principles, worked assiduously to produce relevant quantitative and qualitative data, and made a case for pragmatic as well as visionary steps to achieve a peace dividend.

Our work included an international counterpart from the start. During an early 1990s sabbatical, I spoke in many places around the world about dismantling the cold-war economy. In the process, I found partners to work with in many countries. A fair amount of my work and writing has compared the American experience with that of other countries, the learning going in both directions. In Europe, in particular, our work has resulted in significant contributions to the shaping of strategic thinking about defense economics and trans-Atlantic alliances.

Pace matters in an abrupt downturn such as that associated with deep military-spending cuts in the early 1990s, and that may follow the end of Middle Eastern hostilities as well. Human and physical resources may be rendered useless for long periods unless care is taken to move people into new skills and jobs, to find civilian uses for military technologies, and to offer bridging finance and technical assistance to smaller firms. Our work was aimed at understanding, documenting, and disseminating knowledge about this process and coming up with creative solutions and policy initiatives.

Have we been successful? I wish we could say we permanently dismantled the bulk of the cold war's weapons-making-and-deploying systems. That project is currently in remission because huge increases in military spending associated with the war in Iraq have created an umbrella for continuing old programs. But our work did make major contributions to the institutional and programmatic realization of the peace dividend in the United States. In what follows, I discuss a few of the most obvious achievements of the past decade. Each of these required work with vocal and powerful constituents, and with them we share the credit. Each involved conflict. Each was only a partial success.

First, we helped many communities to understand their crises and to identify and secure transitional assistance. Many were able to help their large and small firms move from military to civilian products and services. Others with military bases planned for and implemented alternative uses of the land, buildings, and personnel. We worked extensively on several regional economies—St. Louis, Long Island, Los Angeles (Oden, Markusen, Flaming, Feldman, Raffel, and Hill, 1996; Oden, Hill, Mueller, Feldman, and Markusen, 1993; Oden, Mueller, and Goldberg, 1994), and Los Alamos/Albuquerque (Markusen et al., 1995). There we educated conversion activists about what was possible and how to frame arguments, raised the visibility of defense conversion efforts through press conferences and public media appearances, and supported legislative and administrative initiatives, many of which made a difference. This locally grounded work was among our most effective because it not only created real civilian jobs but also encouraged large numbers of citizens to demand superior alternatives to the pumping of defense dollars into the local economy. We took these same experiences and disseminated them via a national network of conversion advocates.

Second, we worked with advocates and policymakers to introduce institutional innovations at the federal level. This quickened the pace and quality of conversion. I wrote two opinion editorials in *The New York Times* in the 1990s making the case for significant institutional capacity building (Markusen, 1992a, 1992b). Our work with incoming President Bill Clinton and his team resulted in a new Office of Economic Conversion in the Department of Commerce and a beefing up of the Department of Defense's Office of Economic Adjustment. Our support for and early evaluation of two technology initiatives—the Technology Reinvestment Program (DOD) and the Advanced Technology Program (DOC)—resulted in the strengthening of both through design changes we recommended (Oden, Bischak, and Evans-Klock, 1995). Our work on the national nuclear-weapons labs led to programmatic changes enabling more scientists and engineers to take their ideas and technologies out into the world of commerce and to a more concerted focus on commercialization within the labs themselves.

Third, we worked especially hard on the tough problem of defense workers, many of whom were older, specialized, and clustered in regions hard hit by defense cutbacks. Company mergers and relocations further compounded these problems. We critiqued the entire system of displaced-worker assistance in the United States through the lens of defense workers, stressing the short-term and inappropriate nature of aid and retraining, the absence of anything like a GI bill, and the paltry level of funds committed to existing programs, which were able to serve only 7 percent of those eligible (Mueller et al., 1993). Our insights were welcomed by the new Clinton Department of Labor, which was committed to a major overhaul of workforce development programs and a focus on displaced workers. We continued through the decade to monitor displaced-defense-worker experience and to jawbone the Department of Labor and state and local counterparts on these issues (Powers and Markusen, 1998). We provided intellectual fodder for the bipartisan Congressional assault on "payoffs for layoffs"—billions paid to defense contractors by the Department of Defense to shut plants and cut jobs. That effort failed.

Fourth, the quality and impact of our joint work created opportunities to work face-to-face with elites and policymakers on major issues of American defense procurement and military policy. In 1995, the president of the Council on Foreign Relations in New York approached me to join the council as a senior fellow to run a study group on defense conversion. For the next seven years, which included my early Humphrey Institute years, I ran a lively roundtable that moved from topic to topic, commissioned papers (many of which have had a major impact on Department of Defense and State Department policy), and brought actors with widely divergent views face to face.

As one participant recently said to me, "The day that you see the chief lobbyist for the Mennonite peace movement sitting next to and conversing respectfully if heatedly with the chief strategist for the National Rifle Association on arms-trade issues, you know you are creating a dialogue that matters!" The study included trade unionists, Wall Street investment bankers, defense company executives, local economic development advocates, peace and justice workers, defense economists and political scientists, nonprofits leaders, senior fellows from the military, and policymakers from agencies including the CIA and the United Nations.

National defense consumes an enormous chunk of economic activity. It is complex and poorly understood by the public. Often, our efforts were challenged by unexpected developments. Two examples bear some discussion: 1) aggressive merger bids sapped the commitment of companies to conversion, and 2) tantalizing new government subsidies from foreign arms sales diverted companies' attention from efforts to develop new civilian technologies. We crafted new research initiatives in response to each.

From our work in Los Angeles, we detected the devastating effect of defense company mergers on fragile defense-conversion initiatives. We turned our sights on the character and motivations for these mergers, crafting a trenchant critique of their destructiveness and the role of Clinton's Pentagon in encouraging them (Markusen, 1997b, 1998b, Oden, 1998). I built the intellectual framework for opposing further defense mergers and presented it in policy forums and in major national newspapers (Markusen, 1994, 1997a, 1997c, 1998a). I take some credit for the trend-breaking denial of the Lockheed-Martin/ Northrup-Grumman merger. This policy decision prompted greater diversification among the respective military contractors while preserving more competition in military procurement.

The Clinton administration undercut its own conversion commitment and facilitated arms sales by permitting accelerated exports of the highest-quality weapons and accompanying them with massive new subsidies and promotional efforts. U.S. arms sales zoomed to 40 percent of the world market, one that was imploding in the mid-1990s. I educated myself on arms-trade issues and successfully rebutted claims that arms exports created more American jobs. One troubling development is the increased use of offsets—agreements by sellers of weapons to buy, market, or invest in buyer-country products and services in return for weapons sales. In a Council on Foreign Relations paper, written and widely circulated while I was at the Humphrey Institute and published in 2004 (Markusen, 2004), I demonstrated that the practice of offsets gave away even more jobs to foreign companies and distorted the public-spending decisions of buyer countries while increasing the potential for proliferation and creating an "arms race with ourselves."

A red-letter day came in early 2000, when an admiral in the U.S. Navy with whom I had worked at the Council on Foreign Relations vetoed a major sale of F-16s to Chile on the basis of what he had learned in the study group. My work on this topic resulted in my appointment to the President's Commission on Offsets in International Trade. There we generated important new data on the size and impact of offsets and mapped out the range of policy alternatives before being disbanded via neglect by the new Bush administration (Presidential Commission on Offsets in International Trade, 2001.) Two years later, I gave a plenary talk on this problem at a conference in South Africa. Offsets remain an increasingly serious problem in international trade and economic development.

That heightened militarism is eroding the enormous worldwide peace dividend of the 1990s—invested well in public infrastructure, social services, education, and private capital formation—is disturbing. But investments made with that peace dividend will, of course, continue to pay off. Our work has created a significant template, I believe, for how to move resources from defense into development. Even now, some countries and regions are engaged in this happy activity—demobilizing soldiers and turning them into farmers and workers, creating more efficient and environmentally benign traffic systems from aerospace technologies, and reclaiming landmine-ridden lands for agriculture.

References

Markusen, Ann

1992a   "Department of the Peace Dividend." *The New York Times,* May 18: p. A17.

1994   "Don't Let Mergers Crowd Out Conversion."*Christian Science Monitor,* September 27: p. 18.

1997a   "The Downside of Boeing-McDonnell Merger." *St. Louis Post-Dispatch,* January 5, p. 3B.

1997b   "The Economics of Defence Industry Mergers and Divestiture." *Economic Affairs* 17(4): 28–32.

1997c   "The Foolish, and Costly, Defense Merger Mania." *The International Herald Tribune,* January 11, www.iht.com/articles/1997/01/11/edann.t.php#

1998a   "Global Defense Mergers." *The Christian Science Monitor,* August 5: p. 11.

1998b   "The Post-Cold War Persistence of Defense Specialized Firms." In Gerald Susman and Sean O'Keefe (Eds.), *The Defense Industry in the Post-Cold War Era: Corporate Strategies and Public Policy Perspectives* (pp. 121–46). London: Elsevier Science.

2004   "The Arms Trade as Illiberal Trade." In Jurgen Brauer and J. Paul Dunne (Eds.), *Arms Trade and Economic Development: Theory, Policy, and Cases in Arms Trade Offsets* (pp. 66–88). London: Routledge.

2000   *America's Peace Dividend: Essays on the Achievements of the 1990s and the Challenges Ahead.* New York: Columbia International Affairs Online. (Login required) http://www.ciaonet.org/book/markusen

Markusen, Ann, and Sean Costigan, eds.
1999   *Arming the Future: A Defense Industry for the Twenty-first Century.* New York: Council on Foreign Affairs.

Markusen, Ann, Sean DiGiovanna, and Michael Leary, eds.
2003   *From Defense to Development? International Perspectives on Realizing the Peace Dividend.* London: Routledge.

Markusen, Ann, Michael Oden, James Raffel, and Marlen Llanes
1995   *Coming in from the Cold: The Future of Los Alamos and Sandia National Laboratories.* New Brunswick, NJ: Rutgers University, Project on Regional and Industrial Economics.

Markusen, Ann, Peter Hall, Scott Campbell, and Sabina Deitrick
1991   *The Rise of the Gunbelt.* New York: Oxford University Press.

Markusen, Ann, and Joel Yudken
1992   *Dismantling the Cold War Economy.* New York: Basic Books.

Melman, Seymour
1970   *Pentagon Capitalism: The Political Economy of War.* New York: McGraw-Hill.

1974   *The Permanent War Economy: American Capitalism in Decline.* New York: Simon and Schuster.

1983   *Profits without Production.* New York: Alfred A. Knopf.

1988   *The Demilitarized Society, Disarmament and Conversion.* Montreal: Harvest House.

Mueller, Elizabeth, Jose Cachaza, Jonathan Feldman, Donald Free, Laura Goldberg, Mia Gray, Philip Gregory, and Ann Zeidman
1993   *Retraining for What? Displaced Defense Workers Come Up against EDWAA.* Project on Regional and Industrial Economics, Rutgers University.

Oden, Michael
1998   "Defense Mega-Mergers and Alternative Strategies: The Hidden Costs of Post-Cold War Defense Restructuring." In Gerald Susman and Sean O'Keefe (Eds.), *The Defense Industry in the Post-Cold War Era: Corporate Strategies and Public Policy Perspectives* (pp. 147–52). Oxford: Elsevier Science.

Oden, Michael, Gregory Bischak, and Christine Evans-Klock
1995   *The Technology Reinvestment Project: The Limits of Dual-Use Technology Policy.* New Brunswick, NJ: Rutgers University, Project on Regional and Industrial Economics.

Oden, Michael, Catherine Hill, Elizabeth Mueller, Jonathan Feldman, and Ann Markusen
1993   *Changing the Future: Converting the St. Louis Economy.* New Brunswick, NJ: Rutgers University, Project on Regional and Industrial Economics.

Oden, Michael, Ann Markusen, Dan Flaming, Jonathan Feldman, James Raffel, and Catherine Hill
1996   *From Managing Growth to Reversing Decline: Aerospace and the Southern California Economy in the Post Cold War Era.* New Brunswick, NJ: Rutgers University, Project on Regional and Industrial Economics, February,

Oden, Michael, Elizabeth J. Mueller, and Judy Goldberg
1994   *Life after Defense: Conversion and Economic Adjustment on Long Island.* New Brunswick, NJ: Rutgers University, Project on Regional and Industrial Economics.

Powers, Laura, and Ann Markusen
1998   *A Just Transition? Lessons from Defense Workers' Experience in the 1990s.* Washington, DC: Economic Policy Institute.

Presidential Commission on Offsets in International Trade
2001   Status report of the Presidential Commission on Offsets in International Trade. Washington, DC: Executive Office of the President of the United States, Office of Management and Budget, January 18.

Weidenbaum, Murray
1992   *Small Wars, Big Defense: Paying for the Military after the Cold War.* New York: Oxford University Press.

—10—

Industry Clusters
and Economic Development
in Minnesota

Lee W. Munnich Jr.

The Hubert H. Humphrey Institute of Public Affairs established its State and Local Policy Program (SLPP) in 1991 to fulfill the University of Minnesota's land-grant mission of teaching, research, and outreach. The institute does so by helping public and private leaders and citizens understand and address state and local issues through

- convening . . . to increase discussion and awareness of policy issues
- contributing . . . to produce and integrate new information, ideas, and approaches
- changing . . . to enhance and apply public policy that addresses community needs.

Since its inception, in these several ways, SLPP has helped economic development policymakers in Minnesota and other states, as well as in other countries, to understand their economies and to develop broader-based development strategies for knowledge-based economies.

SLPP has accomplished this through research projects, courses, conferences, and consulting arrangements. It contributed to, among other things, an understanding of industry clusters and their role in economic development. As a senior fellow and the director of SLPP, I have been privileged to help shape the institute's state and local economic and community development research and outreach activities.

In 1992 SLPP convened a national summit on state and local economic development strategies, bringing together innovative thinkers to discuss economic development policy. The sessions reflected the major topics of discussion and debate at the time—whether economic development policy is a zero-sum game, the role of state and local governments in the global economy, the emergence of regional economic development organizations, evaluating economic development programs, and third-wave strategies. Discussion of third-wave economic development strategies was particularly lively. Participants debated about whether economic development strategies were entering a significantly different new phase and whether they would continue to focus on business attraction and retention programs.

In 1997 SLPP conducted another national conference on innovations in economic development, which focused on the use of data in economic development, workforce development policies, and industry clusters as an economic development strategy.

During a discussion at the 1992 economic development summit, one participant commented that she was impressed with the ideas expressed but wondered whether there was a guidebook on how to apply these new approaches. Her question led to a grant from the U.S. Economic Development Administration to develop a benchmarking tool for state and local governments to assess and improve their economic development strategies. More than a hundred economic development professionals, policy thinkers, academic experts, and regional leaders engaged in roundtable discussions, phone conferences, and pilot tests that led to SLPP's 1995 report *Emerging Principles in State and Local Economic Development: A Benchmarking Tool.* State, regional, and local economic development organizations contributed ideas for twenty-four models in different states as examples of the ten emerging principles.

The ten principles—competitiveness, equity, global economy, comprehensive strategy, regional collaboration, industrial focus, customer satisfaction, partnerships, measurement and evaluation, and learning—offer a framework for states and local governments to assess and improve their approaches to economic development. The report has been widely distributed in both hard copy and through the SLPP website <http://www.hhh.umn.edu/centers/slp/> and is used by economic development practitioners seeking to improve their economic development strategies.

One of the ten principles identified in the 1995 report is that economic development strategies must focus on clusters of industries well-suited to an area as opposed to targeting individual firms or businesses. Industry clusters are not a new idea. Many decades ago economist Joseph Schumpeter noted, "Industries tend to cluster in distinct geographic districts, with individual cities specializing in production of narrowly related set of goods." During the 1990s, Harvard Business School's Prof. Michael Porter generated broad interest in industry clusters through his book *Competitiveness of Nations* (1990) and subsequent articles in the *Harvard Business Review.*

Porter examined successful industry clusters throughout the world—the Italian shoe industry, the Dutch flower industry, and the Japanese electronics industry, for instance. His conclusion was that all of these industry clusters were competitive because of innovation and productivity improvement driven by four conditions, which he called the "diamond of advantage":

- factor conditions—such as a specialized labor pool, specialized infrastructure, and sometimes, selective disadvantages that drive innovation
- home demand—local customers who push companies to innovate, especially if their tastes or needs anticipate global demand
- related and supporting industries—competition among local suppliers for related industries, creating a high-quality, supportive business infrastructure, and spurring innovation and spin-off industries
- industry strategy, structure, and rivalry—intense rivalry among local industries that is more motivating than foreign competition, and a local "culture" that influences individual industries' attitudes toward innovation and competition.

In 1994, I initiated a study with the Twin Cities Metropolitan Council of industry clusters in the region. The purposes of the study were to determine which industries were most competitive in the region, whether the Porter "diamond of advantage" applied to these industries, and what the implications for public policy might be. A research team led by the Humphrey Institute and the Metropolitan Council and including economic analysts from the Minnesota Department of Economic Security, the Minnesota Department of Trade and Economic Development, the research office (House Research) of the Minnesota House of Representatives, the City of Minneapolis and City of St. Paul, and Minnesota Technology, Inc., examined a range of possible analytical tools with which to conduct industry cluster study.

The research team settled on a fairly simple and accessible quantitative approach, using location quotients based on ES 202 employment and wage data from the Minnesota Department of Economic Security. (The location quotient is an index for comparing an area's share of a particular activity with the area's share of some basic or aggregate phenomenon.) These location quotients allowed SLPP to examine industry concentration and change in concentration over time and to make an initial assessment of which industries were most important to the region.

The SLPP/Metropolitan Council team initially identified seven industries but decided to focus on four for the study—medical devices, printing and publishing, computers and software, and metal and metalworking. A subsequent study by graduate student Elizabeth Starling focused on the Twin Cities financial services industry.

SLPP supplemented the quantitative analysis with a qualitative approach based on interviews and focus groups with key industry leaders and experts. Using the Michael Porter framework, we developed a set of questions to lead to better understanding of the competitive forces that drive innovation and keep industries viable. The information generated from these interviews and focus groups confirmed the basic Porter arguments in Minnesota and provided a way of understanding the forces that might affect the future growth and competitiveness of each industry.

The medical-devices industry, for example, has deep entrepreneurial roots in the Twin Cities, an extensive network of specialized supplier expertise, and a sophisticated medical community that demands quality and generates interest in new technologies.

The financial services report predicted future mergers of large banks, which occurred a few years later with the mergers of Norwest Bank with Wells Fargo and First Banks with US Bank. The research also confirmed the historical relationship of the University of Minnesota in the early development of the medical-devices industry; its role in the development of the computer and software industry was less significant.

The initial study of the Twin Cities industry clusters led to interest by persons in other Minnesota regions about whether the phenomenon of industry clusters applied to them. Industry clusters are frequently viewed as urban events—agglomeration economies resulting from dense clusters of competing businesses, suppliers, and consumers. While there is strong evidence of agglomeration economies, many successful industries thrive in less densely populated areas and smaller urban centers. Starting with a study of four industry clusters in the southeast/south central region of Minnesota, SLPP examined how clusters worked in non-metropolitan regions. Subsequently, SLPP has conducted industry cluster studies in the southwestern, northwestern, and northeastern regions of Minnesota.

What we learned from these studies is that competitive clusters that have some if not all of the characteristics of a Porter industry cluster exist throughout the state. The characteristics of these clusters include a knowledge base associated with an industry or a specialized part of an industry that has historical roots, competitive advantages, and formal and informal institutional linkages. Examples of these clusters are the recreational-vehicle industry (snowmobiles, all-terrain vehicles, jet skis) in northwest Minnesota, automated manufacturing in Alexandria in west central Minnesota, and the wireless industry in Mankato in south central Minnesota. SLPP studies of clusters in rural and urban areas continue as a basis for economic development, workforce development, infrastructure, and education policies.

The industry-cluster studies have generated interest beyond Minnesota. One interesting development resulted from contact with the University of Minnesota by an economic development representative of a Swiss canton, who had read the 1995 Twin Cities cluster report on Minnesota's medical-devices industry. The representative recommended that the canton, which had related device industries, establish linkages with the Twin Cities. These included sponsorship of a course at the University of Minnesota with the Carlson School of Management and the Institute of Technology, a joint website on medical technology with the university, and several new business relationships. SLPP has now broadened its work to focus on competitive knowledge clusters in rural areas with a particular focus on the role of institutions and entrepreneurship.

The Humphrey Institute's State and Local Policy Program fulfills the University of Minnesota's land-grant mission of teaching, research, and service to the community through convening, contributing through teaching and research, and changing public policy and practice. SLPP's research on industry clusters (as well as other economic development subjects), convening of policy leaders and practitioners, use of its website to disseminate knowledge, and engagement of graduate students in applied research are positive contributions to the field of state and local economic development.

—11—

The Development and Impact
of the Circle Model of Mediation

Tom Fiutak

The process of mediation is to a great degree a hard art rather than a soft science. Mediating means facilitating the communication among parties in a dispute for the purpose of reaching a durable agreement. In theory, the mediator relies on the ability to perceive what is possible and to guide the parties to a point where the parties can judge the value of a mutual agreement. In practice, mediations have moments of clarity interspersed with interpersonal confusion. The Circle Model of Mediation was developed by me and others to enhance the mediator's understanding of both.

The Circle Model of Mediation developed over time. It emerged from a series of unanticipated events and considerations. The simplicity of the symbol provides a cognitive doorway to its practical complexity and a compelling framework for what previously were disjointed phenomena. The abstraction came from the pragmatics I saw before me as a mediator. In retrospect, the theory informed the practice as much as the practice informed the theory. It follows that the model, if successfully understood and applied, will continue to adapt according to this collision of concept and context.

The Essentials of the Circle Model of Mediation

Mediation as Negotiation

The Circle Model of Mediation starts from the premise that mediation is one of several forms of assisted negotiation. Negotiation is, at the core, the nonviolent pursuit of resolving mutually held perceptions of incompatible interests. A problem must be solved. A tool is needed for exchanging perceptions. The Circle Model starts as a problem-solving tool.

Mediation as a Sequencing of Questions

In 1984, Harlan Cleveland, then dean of the Humphrey Institute, asked me to consider responding to a Request for Funding Proposal from the John and Flora Hewlett Foundation to establish a basic research center to study conflict management.

One of my first stops was at the office of Roger Fisher, driving force behind the Harvard Negotiation Project. I no more than sat down in his office than he closed the door, on the back of which hung a pad of news leaf. As I introduced myself by saying we were considering the creation of a sister center to his, he drew a huge circle, divided it into four equal quadrants, wrote *Reality* at the bottom, *Idea* at the top, *What Is* on the left, and *Ought to Be* on the right. We spent the next hour creating the first molecular building blocks for the Conflict and Change Center, starting with the question "What is in reality?" and working our way clockwise to "What ought to be in reality?"

From this beginning, the essence of the Circle Model of Mediation eventually was distilled.

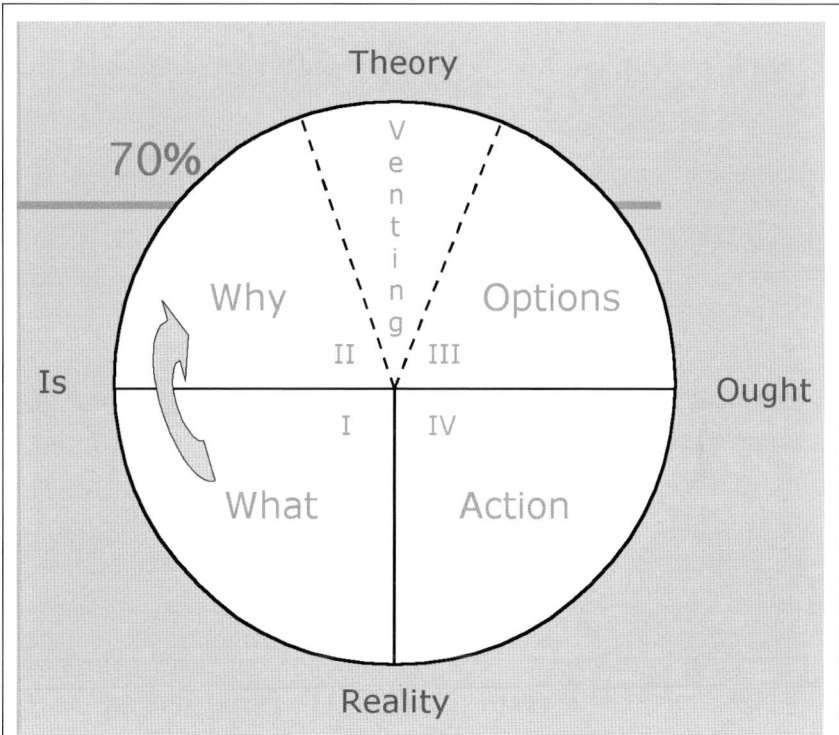

The Circle Model of Mediation is composed of five basic phases:

1. the perceptions of reality that parties choose to bring into the mediation. (Quadrant I, lower left)
2. why these interests are of value and what assumptions lie beneath them (Quadrant II, upper left)
3. the identification of the emotional component of the interests at stake (V-shaped wedge at the top of the circle)
4. which options should be considered should a range of possible agreements exist (Quadrant III, upper right)
5. the action plan for creating a new reality (Quadrant IV, lower right).

Looking for What Is Common among the Variations
In the late 1980s, as cofounder and codirector of the Conflict and Change Center, I was gathering as much mediation training and practice as I could. I found that I needed a conceptual tool to make sense of the variations encountered in the process of mediating.

The main conceptual models at that time revolved around family-mediation dynamics and labor-management negotiations. There was further training for housing-court mediation, conciliation-court mediation, and domestic-abuse mediation, to name just a few. Each model appeared to be geared to a specific context or organizational idiosyncrasy. From one mediation-training session to the next, we would build our awareness of a specialized social context in which mediation could be applied. But we did not yet have a way to express the common activities that trainers mistakenly assumed were understood by all the participants.

Emotional Content within the Mediation—The Venting Wedge
When I was learning mediation, it was taught as a form of diplomacy. In basic texts, the test of a good mediator was the ability to suppress emotional display by the parties. Emotions were seen as a diversion from the process control that is in the realm of the mediator. Yet in the mediations I facilitated and in discussions with colleagues, the processing of emotions within the mediation appeared to be critical junctures leading to breakthroughs toward agreements. The Venting Wedge, placed as a floating wedge in the top half of the Circle Model, became the bridge anchoring the disembodied theory with the emotional reality observed and experienced by mediators around the world.

Examples of How the Model Has Influenced Theory and Practice

My pursuit is to shed light on the fundamental cadence of a mediated event. The Circle Model developed from my need to make sense of what I was experiencing as a mediator. Its development was accelerated by the input from those students and practitioners whose exposure to the model supported their ability to interpret their form of practice. The model was not intended to be the model of mediation. Instead, its purpose is to provide a common conceptual language of practice among mediators, to act as a template against which other mediation models may be analyzed.

For the Mediator

The Circle Model provides a guide for the sequence, transition points, criteria, and role options within the process of mediation. I have never facilitated a mediation that perfectly reflected the conceptual model. Each mediation is a variation of the theory. Rather than a road map, the Circle Model provides an analytical lens indicating where, in the confusion of the moment, the process may be and, more importantly, what may be the next step.

Mediators face an intriguing isolation. Depending on the context in which the mediation is structured, a mediator works in partnership with another mediator or by himself or herself. In the dual model of mediation, the assumption is that the two mediators have worked out between themselves the division of tasks and duties.

The mediators develop a general plan of mediation as well as provide an opportunity to debrief the process once completed, reinforcing mutually agreed-upon behaviors and attempting to extinguish nonproductive ones. In the majority of mediations, a single mediator is used. Once the mediation is closed, the natural course of self-reflection and analysis takes place.

Neither I nor any of the hundreds of other mediators I have met claims to have facilitated the perfect mediation. In the absence of another mediator, given the confidentiality of the mediating arena, the single mediator can use the mental map of the Circle Model as a structured process for reflection and self-debriefing.

In Teaching

Not until I began teaching the process of mediation to others did I recognize my own model. In the process of teaching, I also recognized its weakness.

For the mediator, models serve as interpretive devices to help frame the conditions evolving within the mediation itself. Because these conditions are unpredictable at the micro level, the art of mediation is to sense and respond to the uniqueness of the moment. When the model of the process becomes a rigid structure through which the mediator forces the parties, the model dominates and thereby subverts the interpersonal interaction.

By way of example, when I teach mediation, the final exam is a series of mock mediations that each student must complete using external mediators as role players. Evaluation by the role players is a critical source of assessment regarding the skill of the student. One class finished the role plays and received a resoundingly negative reaction from my evaluators. The evaluators discovered that the students had determined among themselves that the real purpose of the evaluations was to see whether each student could complete the Circle Model within the time allotted. The result was predictable. Instead of the interests of the parties driving the model, the model drove their interests.

In Training

In 1991, I chaired a panel for the International Association of Conflict Management conference in Holland and found myself displaying the model á la Fisher, to mediators from several countries, as a method of visualizing the common aspects of the variety of processes being described. A professor from the University of Paris, Jacques Salzer, was particularly intrigued, for the method provided a cohesive platform for the style of mediation training he had been developing. Through his invitation, over the past eleven years, I have trained lawyers, government officials, consultants, European Union negotiators, community mediators, and judges from France, the Philippines, Poland, Belgium, Germany, Austria, Luxembourg, Switzerland, Hungary, and the Czech Republic.

The Camembert Phenomenon

Yet another indicator of a dynamic model is its ability to mutate according to the needs of the culture applying the concept. To illustrate: In what has to be one of the better examples of cultural adaptation, the French newsletter for the International Association of Mediators has as its logo my five-sectioned Circle Model. They refer to it as "The Camembert."

Several deaf communities have asked me to train as mediators both deaf and hearing members of the staffs in several schools for the deaf in the United States and Canada. The structure of the Circle Model in the visual world of the deaf allows them to reconfigure mediation as a wheel, allowing the consideration of movement and action. The deaf participants transposed the words to pictures of stickmen. The action and processing of each element of the Circle Model became accessible as a functional tool for the youngest of the children.

At a recent presentation in Europe, a gentleman whom I did not know but who had been taught my model approached me during a break and declared that I must change the model. He was a mediator, and as he reflected on his practice and on the Circle Model, he recognized that, while there are five phases to the model, each phase would vary in time and effort depending on the specific dynamics of parties. I agreed wholeheartedly that this insight was consistent with my experience and training and that I should emphasize this concept with greater force. He beamed with pleasure that his interpretation of the Circle Model was authentic, precisely because he had adapted the concepts correctly without being trapped by the structure.

The Circle Model addresses these critical needs. First, as a reflective template, it allows the single mediator to identify and critique his or her experience in mediation. Second, it provides a fundamental rhythm that can be adapted to the specific qualities of multiple mediation arenas. Third, the model has become an effective teaching tool in several ways. The model can be taught as a configuration of the realistic, complex activity students must address in the training for mediation. It provides a conceptual framework that reduces the mystery for those who wish to understand more about mediation in general. Finally, it is a robust communication tool for mediators who wish to learn from the practical experiences of other mediators, as well as a method of describing their own experiences.

Some Positive Results in the Realm of the Common Good
The Circle Model has been applied in ways and places I had not imagined. You send out an idea, and where it takes root is out of your control. I used this model in Berlin, Germany, in 1993 as the keystone lecture for a conference on Preventive Diplomacy, at which 190 East and West Germans had gathered to discuss the reunification of their country. More than three hundred state legislative staff member from across the United States have learned the model through the Legislative Staff Management Institute held at the Humphrey Institute. The Environmental Policy Association in the Czech Republic has been trained in the use of this model to address community environmental disputes. The European Masters, a group in training to accelerate the negotiation acumen of the European Union countries, have requested a second round of training because they have used the Circle Model with success. The teaching of this model to French judges has supported a rapid increase in the use of mediation in the courts.

Pinpointing the connection between an outcome and the Circle Model is more difficult. Yet two examples, one having to do with the public good of a country, the other with the public good of a neighborhood, may suffice.

In 1992, I was invited to meet for a week with an extraordinary coalition of political representatives in the Philippines. Thirty-one men and women, in a coalition sweeping from the country's senate on the far right to the Maoist insurgents and the New People's Army on the left, had agreed to come together to determine which negotiation skills might move the country away from its military stalemate. I was the sole facilitator, and I taught them the Circle Model.

By the end of the week they had agreed that the next round of formal negotiation would take place for the first time outside the country of the Philippines. A year later, I received a handwritten note from one of the coordinators of the coalition. He wrote that, due to political shifts in the Philippines, the coalition had split. But, he added, each side was using the Circle Model to negotiate back to a new coalition.

More recently, a middle-aged woman asked my help with a problem. She was the housing director for a complex of Hmong families. At issue was the apportioning of garden space to each family for use in growing vegetables. Each time a dispute broke out she brought the families into the basement for a negotiated settlement, only to have the emotional energy overwhelm her. She had believed a negotiation must be rational and composed.

I talked with her about the Circle Model of Mediation, saying that my colleagues and I had found that such emotion belongs in the process and is vital to the durability of whatever agreement is struck. The shift is simple: Emotion belongs in a negotiation. When families raise their voices, as long as no threats are made, it is best to allow the venting, then to ask what options there may be. Two weeks later I received a postcard from her with a drawing of the Circle Model on the back, the Venting Wedge colored in red. The script simply read, "It worked, thanks."

Part III

Creating New Institutions

—12—

From Institutional and Policy Design
to Capacity Building:
A Journey through Central and Eastern Europe

Zbigniew Bochniarz

In 1987 a small project—Economic Mechanisms for Environmental Protection in Poland and Other East European Countries—on market based incentives for environmental protection in Central and Eastern Europe (CEE) initiated a journey that led from Poland through seven other CEE countries. The project contributed significantly to institutional and policy reforms and to the human and social capacity-building necessary for the smooth transformation of these countries to civil societies with sustainable market economies.

Run by three faculty members and one graduate research assistant at the Humphrey Institute, the project touched territory still within the "evil empire." Its universal message was to resolve serious environmental problems by sharing academic expertise and the best American experience. Its final accord took place at an international workshop in Poland in September 1989, when the rest of CEE was still under

Communist rule and the Berlin Wall symbolized the deep division between East and West.

The spirit of change, however, was there already, clearly articulated by representatives of CEE countries in their desire for profound institutional change that would lead to democratic political systems providing social justice and sustainable economies. Long, honest discussions among American and CEE participants of the workshop helped to uncover the most needed area of assistance—institutional theory and practice of design, reform, and evaluation. At a critical moment the Humphrey Institute started an assistance effort that has since made it famous in the region.

Since the fall of 1989, which brought freedom to most of the CEE nations, the institute has carried out research through joint American-CEE teams. They have focused on institutional reforms that have improved economic, ecological, and educational systems in the region. Joint in-country and Humphrey Institute teams completed comprehensive planning blueprints containing recommended policies for sustainable development in Poland (1990), Czechoslovakia (1991), Hungary (1992), and Bulgaria (1992).

Three "catalytic" institutions—independent nonprofit research and action centers—were founded (in Warsaw, Prague, and Budapest) to facilitate implementation of the blueprints. These have been in operation since the early 1990s. All these activities and institutions have helped establish working relations with governments, academia, NGOs (nongovernmental organizations, or nonprofits), and businesses in the region. They have fostered design of national environmental institutions such as the Eco-Fund and the Bank for Environmental Protection, in Poland, and shaped environmental and business legislation in several CEE countries. Finally, this work led to the drafting of a regional report on sustainable development for the Earth Summit in Rio de Janeiro in 1992. The report—*Capacities and Deficiencies for Implementing Sustainable Development in Central and Eastern Europe*—

presented an evaluation not only of institutional but also of educational capacities for sustainable development in CEE. One of the most difficult barriers to sustainable development, the report concluded, lay in the unsupportive priorities of the education process. Too much attention, it explained, was devoted to the transfer of knowledge and too little time to the development of appropriate interactive skills and attitudes. For example, managers learned about the environment through the natural sciences but not about how to deal with actual problems. And they were unprepared to apply what they learned.

In addition, the report found severe gaps in modern management and neoclassical economics education, leaving business leaders ill-prepared to design and implement effective sustainable development projects. Furthermore, the academic curricula had basic gaps in environmental economics, natural resource economics, and environmental management.

The report also identified a severe lack of rudimentary market-economy and environmental knowledge among public-sector decision makers. All of these educational shortcomings became painfully obvious during the institutionalization of the market economy and the implementation of new environmental legislation in CEE.

In response to those educational needs, large public-private consortia, led by the Humphrey Institute, developed and delivered these four multiyear educational projects:

- Management Training and Economic Education Program for Poland (1991–2000)
- Environmental Training Project for Central and Eastern Europe (1992–2000)
- Ukrainian Business Strengthening Activity (1999–2002)
- Business Management Education in Ukraine (2002–2005).

These four projects trained more than 42,000 participants in management and economics, providing them knowledge and skills for success in a market economy. All of them received financial support from the U.S. Agency for International Development.

The capacity-building projects not only trained local people but also built the sustainable capacity of local trainers and educators and assisted in institutionalizing modern curricula in undergraduate, graduate, and postgraduate programs at CEE universities and business schools. The first Ukrainian project also helped to produce the latest of the series of blueprints—*Building Management Education in Ukraine: A Blueprint for Action* (2001). This document is the most comprehensive institutional and programmatic reform guide for business-management education ever published in Ukraine.

The first three projects have affected education systems in many ways. Following are the major examples of new institutional arrangements in which the institute and its international partners took the lead:

- establishing new academic units such as the College of Management at the University of Warmia and Mazury (UWM) in Olsztyn, Poland
- institutionalizing new curricula such as the executive master's degree in business administration at Warsaw School of Economics (WSE), executive master's program in agribusiness management, and executive dual-degree master's program in business and public management at UWM
- facilitating accreditation of new management-education programs implemented at WSE and UWM
- introducing eight new executive postgraduate programs—yearlong post-diploma studies at universities partnering with the University of Minnesota: Silesian

University of Technology in Katowice (Poland), Silesian University in Katowice, Kosice Technical University (Slovakia), Miskolc University (Hungary), Economic University in Varna (Bulgaria), and Technical University in Cluj-Napoca (Romania)

- facilitating curricular reforms in management and economics in seven CEE countries by retraining more than two thousand faculty members to develop contemporary course materials and to use interactive teaching techniques
- contributing to the introduction of approximately 2,500 new courses and numerous redesigned and updated existing courses of CEE faculty
- implementing revenue-generating activities, such as executive short courses and executive MBA-type programs, at the CEE centers of excellence
- helping to establish sustainable educational institutions such as the centers for excellence at WSE and UWM and post-diploma studies centers at the above-mentioned CEE universities
- establishing a nongovernmental organization for enhancement of Ukrainian management education—Consortium for Enhancement of Ukrainian Management Education (CEUME)
- facilitating establishment of the Ukrainian Association for Management Development and Business Education
- bringing together all major stakeholders of business management education in Ukraine—governmental officials, business representatives, academic leaders and faculty from public and private universities, students, representatives of NGOs, and donors—through national conferences and regional roundtables

- building partnerships among American, Polish, and Ukrainian faculty and institutions
- initiating a reform movement in Ukrainian higher education, beginning in 1999 with the first national conference of universities with education programs in management and continuing with annual conferences thereafter
- organizing a complex process that included more than 1,400 Ukrainian and foreign participants who produced *Building Management Education in Ukraine: A Blueprint for Action.*

Management-education programs developed out of the project at WSE and UWM are among the best in Poland and all of CEE. For that reason, both Polish universities joined the Consortium for Enhancement of Ukrainian Management Education to share their experience with their Ukrainian partners and to strengthen Ukrainian business-education institutions.

Another distinguishing feature of the Humphrey Institute's projects was the introduction of monitoring and evaluation systems that not only fostered program improvement but also identified achievements. For example, the institute has learned that graduates of its programs have been associated with more than three billion dollars of environment-friendly investment during the past twelve years.

More than fifteen years' experience with institutional reform in countries in transition and eleven years of building human capacity in CEE by the University of Minnesota and its partners has resulted in a solid body of knowledge that the Humphrey Institute can share and replicate. This know-how is summarized in the following principles and practices:

- Offer honest, two-way partnership in designing and delivering educational programs.
- Involve top leaders (presidents, rectors, deans).

- Focus on building a critical mass of faculty at the selected partner institutions. (Experience with Polish and CEE partners suggests that the concept of "critical mass" works effectively and that the size of the trained group depends on the requirements of the joint program. For instance, at most CEE midsize universities, a group of ten to fifteen faculty members could introduce a major undergraduate management program; an MBA required fifteen to twenty faculty members, and a post-diploma studies program, between five and eight.)
- Integrate contents of curriculum and pedagogy. (In addition to updating technical information and fostering the free inflow of information, modern executive training is most effective when it includes teaching integrated process skills, periodic reinforcement through follow-up sessions, and content addressed to local and regional concerns.)
- Establish project monitoring and evaluation at the outset of the reform effort.
- Encourage building personnel, administrative, programmatic, and financial sustainability from the outset. (Project implementation best includes a step-by-step shift of responsibility to the region by decentralizing management and building sustainability through increased use of local trainers, jointly authored publications, and local matching finances.)
- Encourage consulting and applied research in business communities.
- Disseminate countrywide program documents and success stories. (The Humphrey Institute's experience clearly indicates the power of local success stories in overcoming risk-aversion elsewhere in the country of success. Per-

haps even more important is the development of a common vision of reforms needed in a blueprint for action. The blueprint builds a consensus of local stakeholders, who will then support each other in the process of joint implementation. The Humphrey Institute also assisted in developing local think tanks, which as catalytic institutions for change continue the mission of the blueprints by providing applied research, consulting, and policy recommendations. All think tanks established with the assistance of the institute during the past fourteen years are sustainable and have been widely recognized at national and international forums as effective applied-research and advocacy organizations. Another effective dissemination of success stories evolved in the alumni associations of graduates of several of the programs, particularly at WSE and UWM. These are now linked with the University of Minnesota Alumni Association.)

Today, the Humphrey Institute—with six blueprints for institutional and policy reforms implemented in the region, with more than forty-two thousand participants in training activities, with three sustainable graduate and six postgraduate programs and their alumni associated with more than three billion dollars in sustainable investments in Central and Eastern Europe, and with a collaborative network of hundreds of academic, NGO, governmental, and business organizations—is the leader among U.S. universities in facilitating a historic transformation from centrally planned economies with totalitarian political regimes to civic societies with liberal economies, from Warsaw Pact members to NATO members, and finally from the Council of Mutual Economic Assistance (Commecon) to European Union membership.

—13—

The International
Women's Rights Action Watch:
Establishing Global Human Rights Policy

Marsha A. Freeman

Maastricht, The Netherlands, October 2002. Spoons tapped against glasses, the international signal for "Quiet, folks." Prof. Cees Flintermann began what we thought would be a welcome to the group, but instead he began to tell this story:

Almost twenty years ago, a young law lecturer named Loes Brunott inspired her faculty at the University of Maastricht to take on women's human rights as a central topic of its teaching and research. At a time when few law professors acknowledged that women have human rights, Brunott's passion and charisma carried the day. In 1985 she teamed up with a few activist colleagues to spread the word at the Nairobi World Conference on Women—where she, Arvonne Fraser of the Humphrey Institute, and a few other friends from a few other countries decided to start something called the International Women's Rights Action Watch (IWRAW).

Arvonne Fraser brought the idea home to Minnesota, where as a senior fellow at the Humphrey Institute she started to build a program. Loes and the others returned to the Netherlands, Colombia, Brazil, Kenya, and New York and became the core of a network that put women's human rights on the map there, at the United Nations (UN), and in the world. The IWRAW program became the global operations and resource center for work on the Convention on the Elimination of All Forms of Discrimination against Women, the international human rights treaty that outlines government accountability for the status of half the world's people.

The story does not end there. Brunott's faculty continued to host symposia and conferences critical to working out legal issues and methods of applying the convention—most recently in October 2002. And since 1986, IWRAW has helped women, and men who are concerned about women, claim their rights under human rights treaties at the UN and in their own countries.

Loes Brunott died in 1989, and in Maastricht we raised a glass to her and to the continuing legacy of the group of women who, seventeen years earlier in Nairobi, had written it all down on a napkin.

The expert group gathered in Maastricht in 2002 brought IWRAW full circle. One of the American founders, now a law professor in Toronto, was there, as well as a law professor from Botswana, who brought IWRAW into the heart of the action on women and law in southern Africa and into a landmark African sex-discrimination case in 1990. Another, a lawyer from Mauritius, recently elected to the UN Committee on Elimination of Discrimination against Women (CEDAW), was instrumental to IWRAW successes at the Fourth World Conference on Women in 1995. The group included an Australian judge who, as the chair of CEDAW, in 1990 invited IWRAW to provide information on the status of women in countries under review at the UN. IWRAW has become known globally for this activity. The German member of CEDAW who participated in this expert group had become my friend and colleague through her passion for promoting affirmative action as a treaty obligation. And Professor Flintermann had just been elected to CEDAW.

A staff member from the Office of the High Commissioner for Human Rights joined us. At age 32 she represented a new generation of female human rights professionals totally at ease in high-level negotiations at the UN.

The genius of the International Women's Rights Action Watch—and I can say this because I was not at Nairobi but joined IWRAW as staff attorney in 1986, shortly after its founding—was its focus on a human rights treaty and its determination to build a network of people who would pursue work on women's human rights in their own space, on their own terms, and in their own time frames. Unlike those in other human rights groups, IWRAW staff members did not have to sit down every year and ask what hot issue or rogue country they would have to pursue to maintain the interest of their constituents. IWRAW offered an agenda defined in universal human rights treaties, one that belongs in perpetuity to every woman in the world.

That being said, it took some time to build a coherent program within the Humphrey Institute and to enlist donors to support it. For a few years the IWRAW founders gathered informally, in New York or Vienna when CEDAW met, bringing with them colleagues just beginning to learn about the Convention. We talked about what was happening in various countries and chewed over various organizational frameworks. We devised elaborate schemes for "focal points" within each region, which were unworkable because nobody had the time to be a consistent, unremunerated focal point. Eventually we designed a framework for self-sustaining but connected regional programs, focusing on more local levels to spread the knowledge and enlist mutual support for the work.

IWRAW Asia Pacific, launched in 1993 out of this design, has become an enormously successful, independent program reaching across regions from its base in Malaysia. Other regional organizing has fallen victim to the vagaries of regional politics and the scarcity of individuals who can devote the time and energy to launching a major independent program.

Organizationally, IWRAW ultimately has become a resource and communications center that encourages and assists an ever growing and changing network of activists and scholars concerned with making women's human rights real. Its newsletter, published from 1987 to 2000, went out to five thousand activists, organizations, and libraries. Its annual meeting became a highly anticipated event. IWRAW organized and presented at conferences and trainings and consultations all over the world. As access to e-mail and to the World Wide Web has grown—today we receive e-mails from places accessible ten years ago only by telegraph—communications has become a core activity.

IWRAW's success is based as much on timing as on talent. Like all social movements, the international women's human rights movement took off because of a confluence of actors and factors. In 1990 three Australian law professors published a groundbreaking law-review article documenting and explicating women's invisibility in the human rights world. Several American activists published important articles in more accessible journals and organized projects to promote women's human rights internationally in media, in conferences, and at the UN. A few had the luck and insight to participate in the early stages of preparation for the 1993 World Conference on Human Rights—and got women on the agenda. Major international human rights groups started "women's projects." When we heard in 1992 that Aryeh Neier, then the executive director of Human Rights Watch, wanted to call that organizaton's new women's project "Women's Watch," Arvonne Fraser informed him that since our newsletter was titled *Women's Watch* he might want to reconsider—and he did.

When the UN announced its decision to hold the Fourth World Conference on Women in Beijing in 1995, Fraser moved into high gear. She had been involved in all three of the earlier women's world conferences, and she played a major role in the U.S. delegation at Copenhagen in 1980. She was deeply engaged in the Nongovernmental Organizations Forum at Nairobi in 1985. At the annual IWRAW gathering with international colleagues in New York in January 1992, about a dozen of us began to strategize. All except Fraser were new to the world-conference process. Her response to our questions about how it works was typical and accurate: "You decide what you want to do and talk to some donors, and [spinning her arms around each other in a helix motion] it happens!"

There was, of course, more to it than that. The growing global network of activists concerned with women's human rights—moving beyond thinking of women as beneficiaries of development—was not going to be satisfied with yet another collection of statements about women's problems and going forth and doing better. Many American activists had been involved in the 1992 World Conference on Sustainable Development (Rio), the 1993 World Conference on Human Rights, and the 1994 International Conference on Population and Development. We learned how to work these conferences, lobbying governments on issues to be acknowledged and addressed in the official declarations rather than just talking to each other in nongovernmental "forums."

Within the IWRAW program we saw Beijing as a burden we could not avoid and as an opportunity we could not miss. It consumed most of our energy for three years and took a great deal of money to execute well. We came close to psychosis from dealing with the obstructionist and controlling Chinese government. But the conference provided an opportunity to bring hundreds of women into the inner workings of a large UN event. To this day, the legacy of Beijing lies not in its Platform for Action—although at the time it seemed a victory to have that document built on a human rights framework—but in the enormous growth in confidence and skills in the international women's movement, especially in the global south and the former Soviet bloc.

Arvonne Fraser retired from the Humphrey Institute in 1993 and was appointed U.S. ambassador to the UN's Commission on the Status of Women during these preparatory years. I became IWRAW director. We found ourselves literally working the same issues on opposite sides of the street.

While all this was happening, we continued to work with CEDAW, bringing scores of women into the UN human rights process and building a serious presence for women and the IWRAW program. CEDAW experts came to rely on the information in our reports for their reviews of government actions under the CEDAW convention. It used our issue analyses as the basis of policy statements—General Recommendations—adopted as guides to interpreting and applying the Convention. Activists came to rely on IWRAW's information and technical assistance—frequently provided in one-on-one communications, at first by phone or fax and now by e-mail—to learn how to gain access to the human rights review system and how to frame their issues and arguments.

By the late 1990s CEDAW had come to expect activists from reporting countries to be at its sessions. Women's groups were regularly preparing written reports for CEDAW to use in reviews. Many governments routinely consulted with their own female citizens in preparing for CEDAW reviews. With CEDAW help, women had claimed their space in the CEDAW process. We could move on to claiming women's space in the human rights processes not explicitly labeled "for women."

Despite opportunities suggested by the adoption of resolutions and "mainstreaming" programs at the UN since 1993, few women have attempted to use human rights processes other than those of CEDAW to claim their rights. On the UN side, only a few treaty experts have been interested in considering the specific human rights situation of women. Believing that full recognition of women's human rights would not be achieved until they were brought to the attention of experts and government officials whose jobs were not labeled "women," IWRAW started in 1994 to draw attention to women's claims and issues under some of the other treaties. By 1999 we had succeeded: the chair of the Committee on Economic, Social and Cultural Rights (CESCR) invited IWRAW to assist CESCR in developing its formal policy on equality issues.

The International Covenant on Economic, Social, and Cultural Rights is important to women all over the world, as it requires governments to deliver on rights to health, education, employment equality, an adequate standard of living, and the benefits of scientific research. IWRAW had been reporting to the CESCR on women's status in countries under review and assisting women from these countries in using that treaty and the monitoring process. IWRAW assisted CESCR in drafting the General Comment on Equality between Men and Women, the policy statement that will establish a standard for government reporting and CESCR's reviews. Prof. Virginia Bonoan Dandan, CESCR's chair, came to Minneapolis to work with us on the draft in August 2002 and August 2003. After a series of internal procedural delays, the General Comment was adopted in May 2005. The General Comment project provided the opportunity to use everything we have learned about the policy and the politics of human rights to open a new avenue for women to claim their rights.

The ironies of history and the state of the economy placed the IWRAW program at a crossroads as this project ripened. With dramatic changes in the funding base for women's human rights work and in the economic structure of the university, the form and size—but not the heart—of the IWRAW program is changing. The transition remains a work in progress.

I am proud of the accomplishments of IWRAW. I cannot imagine having participated in anything more rewarding over the past eighteen years. I did not do it alone: My gratitude goes to Arvonne Fraser, who shared the dream. The shared passion of friends in Botswana, Bangladesh, Colombia, Bulgaria, Georgia, Japan, Israel, Tanzania, Chile, Egypt, and at least fifty other countries moved the dream closer to reality. Sharon Ladin established our country reporting program. Her successor, Kasia Polanska, brought grace, energy, and international style to the work. Our committed student research assistants included a remarkable list of Cram-Dalton international scholars. Valerie Zamberletti was the heroine of Beijing and a tireless friend and negotiator. Linda McFarland held us together for six of our more adventurous years.

Special thanks to Medora Woods and to the late Kay Cram and the Hon. Earl Larson, who supported the International Women's Rights Action Watch as friends and benefactors, because they believed.

—14—

An Agenda for the States

John E. Brandl

How can free people bring themselves to accomplish public purposes? The very reason for which government exists—to keep people from taking advantage of each other—implies a need to consider whether government-funded programs operate satisfactorily or not. Those responsible for enacting and administering them can at times be expected to look out for their own interests, which may or may not coincide with public purposes.

For twenty years and more my professional work, both within the academy and in public affairs, has attended the development, explication, and partial enactment of a policy agenda for the bulk of what state governments do—namely, provide services. My agenda emerged as the result of several influences: I was brought up in a Catholic family and community, studied economics, and held responsible positions as a young professional in the Departments of Defense and of Health, Education and Welfare (the two largest American bureaucracies). I came to understand that a major part of my role as a state legislator was the design of effective public services. And numerous trips to the formerly Communist countries of central and eastern Europe helped me to see more clearly the inefficacy of much governmental bureaucracy in the United States.

I have articulated this policy agenda in newspaper columns, academic articles, a book, an advisory report to a governor, and in several pieces of legislation. The Hubert H. Humphrey Institute of Public Affairs—which attracts persons seeking to be of service, encourages its members to cross disciplines, and fosters the application of academic research to public affairs—has been the ideal base from which to do this work.

So *how* does a free people best accomplish public purposes? This is the governance question. James Madison's words in *The Federalist Papers* (No. 51) are at least as pertinent today as they were when he urged ratification of the Constitution: "If men were angels, no government would be necessary. If angels were to govern men, neither external nor internal controls on government would be necessary. In framing a government which is to be administered by men over men, the great difficulty lies in this: you must first enable the government to control the governed; and in the next place oblige it to control itself. A dependence on the people is, no doubt, the primary control on the government; but experience has taught mankind the necessity of auxiliary precautions."

First among these precautions is competition, the institutionalizing of countervailing forces. In markets and government, properly constructed competitive arrangements constrain people from taking advantage of others. As Madison put it: "Ambition must be made to counter ambition . . . This policy of supplying, by opposite and rival interests, the defect of better human motives, might be traced through the whole system of human affairs, private as well as public . . . The constant aim is to divide and arrange the several offices in such a manner as that each may be a check on the other."

Madison would be puzzled—probably alarmed—that the "policy of supplying by opposite and rival interests, the defect of better human motives . . . divid[ing] and arrang[ing] the several offices in such a manner as that each may be a check on the other" has not been extended to what is now much the greater part of government—the bureaucracies of the executive branch. A government bureau is an organization funded not by the sale of its products to willing recipients but by lump-sum grants from a legislature. Typically, a government bureau is also a monopoly—that is, it is not subject to the precaution Madison believed essential in "the whole system of human affairs, private as well as public." A government bureau may receive its funding whether or not it accomplishes its purpose.

 Those working in such an organization may or may not be inclined or induced to accomplish the intended goal. Even teachers, people doubtless drawn to their profession by idealistic impulses, sometimes unwittingly but systematically sabotage public purposes. A recent study of the effect of monies appropriated for years by the State of Minnesota specifically for the education of poor children found in the junior high schools of Minneapolis an inverse relationship between the number of low-income students in a school and the amount of money spent there.

The explanation is this: Teachers with the most seniority, given the opportunity to teach where they liked, generally chose the more comfortable schools. The bulk of the budget followed not the students but the experienced teachers. Old-timers chose schools with few poor children but were paid higher salaries than newcomers, and the children became an afterthought. Our founders did not foresee the mammoth service efforts of contemporary government. Neither they nor others since have given sufficient heed to their satisfactory operation.

Once persuaded that insufficient "precautions" characterize government in our time, I found that concern, the governance question, evolving as the core subject of my professional life: How can we design government programs to direct the behavior of the implementing individuals toward successful operation?

The challenge seems both obvious and serious, but even the statement of it infuriates many government workers—who wish to see themselves and to be seen by others as spontaneously altruistic. Perhaps a nation can survive, but as the Minneapolis story illustrates, government surely cannot accomplish much if it operates on the assumption that, unlike everyone else, public employees consistently look out not for themselves but only for the recipients of their services.

This work goes against the grain for others too. Much academic research, especially in public-policy schools, proceeds from the implicit assumption that those making and carrying out policy do so in the interest of the public. Analysts are assumed to determine dispassionately the outcomes of various courses of action. These they present to policymakers who also, implicitly, are assumed to embody the public interest. In this way of thinking, policymaking is construed as choosing among alternatives. Whether the alternatives are objectively delineated or whether policymakers choose in the public interest are questions often ignored.

Similarly, management is typically taught from the implicit assumption that its students are public-spirited persons merely in need of skills. The public provision of services is rarely characterized by careful attention to the governance question. We depend on spontaneous industry on the part of public employees or systematic oversight by politicians.

This inattention explains the main finding of evaluation research over the past several decades. On average, for many government services, there is little relationship between the amount of money spent and the results achieved. Some schools, road construction projects, solid-waste facilities, libraries, bus systems, and so forth, are strikingly effective at turning spending into productive outcomes, but others simply are not. The public schools, monopoly bureaus, are the biggest object of state government expenditure and the best illustration of the point. They spend two, three, or four times as much per student, after adjusting for inflation, as they did thirty or forty years ago. Yet no one can claim that they produce corresponding improvements in children's learning.

Even identifying and advertising the characteristics of successful government programs do not regularly lead to those features being applied elsewhere. (At one time I held a subcabinet position in Washington, responsible for planning, budgeting, and evaluation of the education programs of what was then the U.S. Department of Health, Education, and Welfare. I understood my job as identifying through research and evaluation the distinguishing features of particularly effective schools and approaches to teaching. Later I realized that though we found and promulgated many effective methods and tactics, they were not regularly picked up and applied.) The unexamined presumption behind much policy research is that the knowledge it produces will be put to use. In fact, much of it is ignored. People do not necessarily do what they know.

Finding out what works is not enough. Policymaking must reside not in priority setting, information generation, or budget allocation, but in designing arrangements such that the people assigned to carry out public responsibilities are inclined to do whatever it takes to accomplish them.

The first step in improving public services is to subject them to competition because no one group—not royalty or people wealthy or poor, not businesspeople or government employees, not political liberals or conservatives—may be assumed to be consistently selfless and thus beyond the need for systematic precaution.

Of course, humans are not merely self-interested. Too-rigid adherence to the notion that people look out for themselves may blind one to the possibilities of other-mindedness. But do people dependably transcend self-interest? Are there circumstances in which people consistently act altruistically? Is harnessing self-interest by competition the only reliable policy, the only way of aligning private and public objectives? Or are there policies ensuring that people regularly act spontaneously in the interest of others?

Communitarianism is the conviction that humans are not autonomous, self-interested individuals, but rather social creatures, whole only in groups and devoted to others in those groups. The communitarian vision is that people act not out of narrow self-interest but in the interests of the larger group.

Some communitarian hopes must be recognized as commendable but sentimental. Construing a whole state or the entire country as a community, even as a family, is common in political rhetoric. But this understanding lacks persuasiveness and dependability. Indeed, government exists largely because we do not treat others in the polity in the way we treat members of the family. True, we sometimes are inspired to work towards the public interest. This society needs more of that, but as the American founders knew, constructing policy on the assumption of consistent altruism from citizens is folly. Such an assumption puts all at the mercy of those who are not so honorably inclined.

Still, in some circumstance, people act to benefit others. Certain groups, such as families and religious organizations, sometimes called mediating communities, are able to draw from many people ultimate commitment and consistent action in the interests of those with whom they associate. Perhaps other organizations—neighborhoods and ethnic associations, for example—have the same effect. Government bureaus sometimes, but rarely, possess that quality.

The possibility of consistent altruism within mediating communities suggests that government might meet more of its responsibilities not through private firms or through bureaus but through those communities. Whether a tendency to effectiveness exists for any particular organization is, of course, an empirical question. Government should identify and use the organizations that consistently achieve public purposes.

Neither competition nor community meets public purposes without proper design. Much may go awry in competitive arrangements or purported communities. But if policymakers are serious about public services, they must see their roles not as mere budget allocators, exhorters, or overseers but also, and centrally, as designers of arrangements that achieve the benefits of competition and community while diminishing their drawbacks.

While every piece of legislation is a group effort—and by no means do I claim sole credit for laws that embody the understanding of the policymaking advanced here—I was chief sponsor of several such laws passed by the Minnesota Legislature. The Family Subsidy Program gives a grant to the parents of disabled youngsters choosing to care for the child at home rather than in a state-run hospital. The Minnesota State Grant Program gives low- and middle-income students funds to use at whichever Minnesota college, public or private, they choose to attend. The Minnesota Family Investment Program provides government funding for training and childcare while offering financial incentives for its participants to gain skills and thus become self-supporting.

What are the prospects for an agenda of competition and community? A growing body of empirical research supports such an agenda. And unless the states make greater use of such policy instruments, citizens dissatisfied with what they are getting for their money will become increasingly unwilling to provide tax revenues. This is a sobering prospect for those of us who hold that the states have grand and noble responsibilities.

—15—

Evolving Perspectives on Long-Term Care: Aging and Disability Approaches to In-Home Services

Nancy Eustis

How we think about and provide long-term care has changed radically in the past twenty-five years. The Hubert H. Humphrey Institute of Public Affairs has contributed through its research to two transformations in service provision—a movement from care in nursing homes to services at home in the 1970s and 1980s and a current trend toward consumer-directed long-term care. The former represents an approach of the aging field and the latter an approach of those concerned with disability, to long-term care.

Alternatives to Nursing Homes and an Aging Approach
When I began my work in long-term-care research with a summer job in a retirement home in 1963, the predominant stereotype for the care of frail or disabled elders was residence in a nursing home. At that time, I was probably typical of my peers in that I had no friends

or relatives who needed long-term care. The fields of gerontology and medical sociology, which I subsequently studied in graduate school, were virtually unknown.

By the time the Humphrey Institute was established in 1977, policymakers had become concerned about the rising public costs of nursing homes and numerous accounts of poor care. These concerns plus the increased visibility of older persons' preference for help in their own homes prompted a search for cost-effective alternatives to nursing-home care. A number of studies ensued, comparing outcomes and costs of nursing-home and in-home services. I conducted one of the earlier of these in collaboration with two Humphrey alumni, Jay Greenberg and Sharon Patten. Our research was intended to inform policies of the Minnesota Board on Aging (then called the Governor's Citizens Council on Aging) pertaining to the promotion of in-home service.

The research compared costs and effectiveness of nursing-home and homecare, using data from approximately five hundred residents of nine nursing homes and more than four hundred clients of five homecare agencies. Our findings, reported in 1980, confirmed that homecare can be less expensive than care in a nursing home but demonstrated that cost savings (if any) depend on the extent of the client's functional impairment and whether or not the client lives with someone. We also found evidence of somewhat greater life satisfaction among respondents who lived at home but not among all categories of homecare clients.

This study contributed to an expanded understanding of the comparative costs of these two modes of long-term care and of how homecare often involves shifting costs to lower levels of government and from government to user. It was also one of the first to use measures of ability to perform activities of daily living. Numerous subsequent studies demonstrated and evaluated in-home services as an alternative to nursing homes. Both Greenberg and Patten participated in a national comparison of in-home and nursing-home services, the so-called channeling demonstration.

Greenberg and other Humphrey alumni participated in research on additional approaches to controlling costs of long-term homecare. Greenberg, then a researcher at Brandeis University, played a pivotal role in a national test of managed long-term care. Another Humphrey student, Diane Justice, authored a key study of twelve states that used centrally managed state budgets and case management to control home and community-based services (HCBS) costs. (Justice recently served as the deputy assistant secretary for aging in the U.S. Department of Health and Human Services.)

By the end of the 1980s, most states sponsored statewide HCBS programs for disabled or chronically ill elders who would otherwise be in nursing homes, although nursing-home care continues to receive more than 80 percent of state long-term-care funding. Typically HCBS includes case management provided by the county and services purchased from homecare agencies and other community programs such as, for example, adult daycare.

Consumer-Directed Services, a Disability Approach

In contrast, younger persons with disabilities advocate for the use of public funds to hire directly an assistant of their choice rather than be limited to agency-provided services. They argue that the disabled individual knows his or her needs better than a physician, nurse, or case manager. The consumer-directed approach emphasizes peer support and training in management skills for those directing their services.

I became aware of the views of younger persons with disabilities after being paralyzed as a result of being injured in an automobile accident. Suddenly I was one of "them," a person with a disability, who at age forty needed long-term care, either at home or in a nursing home.

Several years later, Lucy Rose Fischer, a gerontologist then on the faculty of the University of Minnesota's Department of Sociology, and I collaborated on a small, qualitative study of relationships between homecare clients and their paid caregivers. This research proved to be one of the first empirical comparisons of disability and aging approaches as well as an early exploration of the appropriateness of a consumer-directed approach for older persons. We interviewed a sample of working-age adults with disabilities as well as persons over age sixty-five. We also included workers who were employees of homecare agencies and independent providers, that is, workers hired directly by the client.

Our findings illustrated some typical differences in service use between younger and older homecare users. In our study, almost twice as many consumers under age sixty hired an independent provider as did those who were sixty or older. More of the older respondents reported that physicians or other medical professionals were involved in the decision to get services. Younger consumers were also more likely to report training, supervising, and praising or criticizing their workers.

We also found that, although they used different terms than the younger respondents, approximately one-third of the older clients took charge of their homecare arrangements and services. They too used independent providers or played an active role in getting information and communicating with a homecare agency about the selection of workers and their performance. In our study, older clients who took charge in three or more ways tended to be younger (in their sixties or seventies) and without family, to have been disabled longer, and to be more medically stable.

A few years later I served as a guest coeditor of a journal issue entitled *Aging and Disability: Seeking Common Ground*, which explored the application of a disability-and-independent-living perspective to the field of aging. The volume, later published as a book of the same title (Amityville, NY: Baywood, 1992), contained accounts of a number of collaborations between aging and disability experts on a variety of topics. They included geriatrics and physiatry (medical rehabilitation), services for aging persons with developmental disabilities (particularly those with cognitive impairment), and consumer-directed services for younger and older persons with primarily physical disabilities.

In late 1993 I took a leave from the university to accept an appointment as a special assistant in a newly formed Office of Disability, Aging, and Long-Term Care Policy (ODALTCP) in the U.S. Department of Health and Human Services. Researchers and policy analysts in this office had developed the long-term-care provisions–including a consumer-directed option—of then-President Bill Clinton's proposed health-reform legislation. I joined them in developing several major studies to test the effectiveness of consumer-directed long-term care and its appropriateness for older consumers. Findings from one of these, a study of in-home supportive services for the elderly and disabled in California as reported by Benjamin and Mathias in 2001, were largely consistent with the Eustis-Fischer data showing that medically stable, younger seniors were more likely to use independent providers than were seniors not as young or healthy.

I also developed and served as project officer for a survey of state programs providing supportive services to consumers who manage their own services. These include services of so-called fiscal intermediary organizations (for help with payroll taxes and workers' compensation) and of supportive intermediary organizations that may offer training for consumers in management skills, worker training, assistance with locating appropriate workers, and so forth. Other efforts included a grant by the Department of Human Services to the National Council on the Aging and the World Institute on Disability to establish the Institute on Consumer-Directed Services and participation in coalition building among national organizations focused on aging or disability.

After returning to the Humphrey, I headed a small demonstration and evaluation project concerned with the Minnesota Consumer Support Grant (CSG) program, established by the legislature in 1995.

The CSG program provides a cash grant equal to a portion of the cost of the services the participating consumer has been receiving as a beneficiary of an existing publicly funded long-term-care program. The consumer may use his or her grant to purchase a variety of services and supplies or equipment, including paying a relative or neighbor for services provided.

With grants from the Robert Wood Johnson Foundation and the University of Minnesota's Center for Urban and Regional Affairs, project staff from the university and the Department of Human Services developed supports for CSG participants in obtaining and managing their long-term-care services. These included a consumer newsletter and a toll-free help line as well as consumer training manuals. We also conducted an exploratory evaluation of the first thirty months of county implementation and consumers' experience with the program.

Interviews were conducted with twenty-five of the twenty-nine participants enrolled in the program in late 1999. Their experiences illustrate the advantages of consumer direction; their scarcity indicates barriers to this approach. The cash grants that these respondents received ranged from $231 to $4,000 per month. Respondents used up to 70 percent of their grants to cover costs other than personal-assistance or home-health services. Seniors most frequently purchased medications. Families used a part of their grants for therapies, adaptive clothing and equipment, or training for the parents. Most of those who hired a caregiver with funds from the grant hired someone they knew, including relatives.

All of the respondents indicated satisfaction with the CSG program, with most reporting that they were "very satisfied." They said they were more in control of their lives and their services and that they or their family member had more appropriate and/or better quality services. These findings, though obviously of limited generalizability, are consistent with data from much larger studies.

Our small project proved most useful in the support and visibility it provided the CSG program in Minnesota. The program is now much larger. More important, the Department of Human Services is now implementing a consumer-directed option for several of its Medicaid-funded in-home service programs for various categories of persons with disabilities.

By 2001, programs with consumer direction had been implemented in more than half of the states of this country. At home in Minnesota, the Long-Term Care Commission's final report, January 2001, proposed a long-term-care system serving older Minnesotans that "empowers consumers . . . [provides] consumers with useful information about long-term-care options and provider performance . . . [and involves] consumers in the planning, evaluation, and decision-making for long-term care, so that service design is driven at all levels by consumer needs and preferences."

Reference

Benjamin, A.E, and R.E. Mathias
2001   "Age, Consumer Direction, and Outcomes of Supportive Services at Home." *The Gerontologist 41*(6): 632–42.

—16—

An Idea Whose Time Has Come

Joe Nathan

It started with people, a napkin, and a pen. "It," in this case, is the charter idea—an idea that developed in Minnesota and expanded around the country. The Humphrey Institute played five major roles in this movement.

What led to the nation's first charter-public-school law? The charter idea developed from previous Minnesota experience with public-school choice. Since the early 1970s, the state's two largest school districts, Minneapolis and St. Paul, have offered options within their districts. And during the 1980s, the legislature adopted several statewide public-school-choice programs.

At a 1988 conference convened by the Minneapolis Foundation, several school-reform activists met one evening after hearing Al Shanker, president of the American Federation of Teachers, and Sy

Fiegel, one of the architects of the East Harlem public-school-choice plan. Fiegel had described East Harlem's efforts to increase student achievement and reduce discipline problems. He, along with then-superintendent Anthony Alvarado and a few others, decided to ask teachers for ideas about new, small "schools within schools," as an option available to students and educators. The results of this program were encouraging.

Shanker described the frustrations many teachers felt in school systems. He contended, for example, that many teachers who try to create schools within schools are treated like traitors or outlaws for daring to move outside the lockstep and do something different. Their initiators had to move heaven and earth to get school officials to authorize them, and if they managed that, they could look forward to insecurity, obscurity, or outright hostility.

After hearing Shanker and Fiegel, five people met: Barbara Zohn, president of the Minnesota Parent-Teacher-Student Association (PTSA); Elaine Salinas, education program officer of the (Minneapolis-St. Paul) Urban Coalition; Ted Kolderie, a former journalist and director of the Citizens League, a respected Minneapolis-based public policy group; Ember Reichgott, a Democratic state senator from a Minneapolis suburb; and this author.

This group had worked closely with other Humphrey Institute faculty on legislative initiatives expanding school choice. These included Minnesota's

- Post Secondary Enrollment Options (PSEO) law (1985), allowing high-school juniors and seniors to attend colleges and universities, with state funds following the students
- Area Learning Centers and High School Graduation Incentives (1987), allowing twelve-to-twenty-one-year-old students who are not succeeding to attend a public school

outside their district or to attend a private nonsectarian school with a contract from a local school board

- Open Enrollment (1988), allowing students ages five to eighteen to move across district lines as long as the receiving district has room and the transfer does not harm efforts to racially integrate schools.

The five people agreed that while Minnesota families had power to choose among public schools, they had few choices. Few school districts had yet decided to provide different kinds of schools from which families could select.

For several years I had been urging that groups of parents and teachers be allowed to create new options within public education. Alternative school groups around the nation were promoting this idea.

The Minnesota coalition thought the state could not just rely on local school districts to offer options. After all, school boards already had the power to offer different kinds of schools, and less than a handful of Minnesota's more than four hundred districts were doing so. Moreover, a number of the options in Minneapolis and St. Paul had significant waiting lists, and the districts did not seem eager to replicate those successful schools.

The group also had seen the value of Minnesota's PSEO law, helping thousands of students and stimulating improvements in the K–12 system. So the group felt that it was critical to give parents and teachers a way to get approval of new schools outside the existing district system.

Shanker had mentioned the word *charter*, which he picked up from New England educator Ray Budde. For fifteen years Budde had been urging school districts to do what European kings had done for explorers—give them a "charter" to explore.

Expanding on this notion, the Minnesotans wrote down these ideas on a napkin:

- public-school options
- more responsibility in exchange for more autonomy
- use of a contract to list explicit goals, responsibilities, and expectations, plus waivers from local labor/management contracts and most existing state rules and regulations
- some group other than a local board to authorize the pioneering educators.

The charter was not a prescription for curriculum or a set of recommendations about how schools should be designed. It went to the heart of how states provide public education. As Kolderie wrote in a paper widely regarded as the founding document of the movement: "The states will have to withdraw the Exclusive." That is, the states will have to permit groups beyond local school boards to authorize public education. (See Nathan, 1998, for a more detailed history).

What Is the Charter Idea?

The group mentioned above developed the following ideas, which have formed the basis for charter legislation:

1. The state will give more than one publicly accountable organization the power to authorize or sponsor new public schools. This could include the State Board of Education, local school boards, cities, public universities, county boards, and so forth.
2. The school is public. It is nonsectarian. It may not charge tuition. It may not have admissions tests of any kind. It must follow health and safety regulations.
3. Existing public schools may convert to charter status if a majority of the teachers in the school votes to convert.
4. The contract specifies improvements in student achievement that the school must produce to renew its contract.

5. There is an up-front waiver from rules about curriculum, management, and teaching. States may specify student outcomes and state tests.

6. The charter school is a school of choice. Faculty, students, and families choose it.

7. The school becomes a discrete entity. Teachers, if employees, have full rights to organize and bargain collectively. But their unit is separate from any district bargaining unit.

8. The full per-pupil funding allocation moves with the student. If the state provides extra appropriations for students from low-income families or with disabilities, these monies also follow the students.

9. Participating teachers are protected and must be given new opportunities. Teachers may take a leave from their public-school systems and retain seniority. They may continue to participate in their local or state retirement programs. New teachers may join state retirement programs.

Growth of the Charter Movement

In 1991, the Minnesota Legislature adopted many, but not all, of these ideas. The legislature agreed to authorize up to eight new schools and to offer these schools waivers from most state regulations in exchange for responsibility for improving achievement over three years. The legislature insisted, however, that only local school boards could sponsor or authorize charters. And it insisted that the state board of education review each charter application after the school board approved it.

Since 1991, a number of changes have been made to Minnesota's charter law. Several of the most important are summarized in Table 1. These include the following.

1. The number of charters permitted has expanded dramatically.
2. The state has adopted the original idea, which was to allow

people who wanted to create new schools—or convert existing ones—to get permission from a local school board or some other group.

3. The state has committed millions of dollars to help charter public schools obtain buildings in which to operate. That's because unlike district schools, charter public schools may not levy taxes to construct, lease, rehab, or equip buildings.

Table 1: Evolution of Minnesota's Charter Law

Year	Number of Charters Permitted	Sponsors	Lease Aid*
1991	8	Local school boards	$0
2005	Unlimited	Local school boards, universities, intermediate school districts, foundations, nonprofit organizations registered with the state with $2 million end-of-year fund balances.	$1,200/pupil or 90 percent of a building lease, whichever was less. In 2005 more than $20 million.

*Funds used to help pay for the lease of a charter school building.

In addition, forty states, as well the District of Columbia, have adopted the charter idea. Not all of these laws, however, are true to the original charter ideas, outlined above. Nationally, the number of charter public schools in operation grew from one in 1992 to almost 3,400 in the 2004–05 school year, serving almost a million students.

A variety of research shows that charters are helping students all over the nation. In some places, the chartering idea is helping stimulate improvements in existing school districts. That's why, as the National Governors Association (NGA) and the Center for School Change (CSC) noted in 2005:

Many policymakers have begun giving families and students greater choice in education options. They believe that different education options can help meet the goals of improved student achievement and higher graduation rates, meet No Child Left Behind (NCLB) requirements to offer choice options, encourage innovation and improvement across the education system, satisfy parental demands for options, and reduce segregation by race and income. (NGA/CSC, p. 2)

Humphrey Institute Role in the Charter Movement
Humphrey Institute staff members played five key roles in the charter movement, summarized below.

1. Helping develop the idea. As noted above, I helped propose the charter idea's key elements.
2. Providing information to state legislatures interested in the idea. Twenty-one legislatures and three Congressional committees asked me to share information about the charter idea.
3. Conducting research about the movement. One of the central roles of a university is to examine ideas and suggest ways they might be refined and improved. The Humphrey Institute's Center for School Change has done this in several ways.

   In cooperation with the Education Commission of the States, the center undertook the first national survey of charter-school directors and found, among other things, that lack of startup money was viewed as the single greatest barrier to creating charters. Federal officials responded with startup funds. CSC staff and a graduate-student research assistant carried out perhaps the first national study looking closely at charter-school evaluations in several states. This study found that though charter schools can improve student achievement, assessment within charters in some cases was so spotty that it could not identify whether student achievement was being enhanced.

Still another CSC study found that the average charter school in Minnesota received $1,000 less in public funds than did district-run schools, partly because they received little or no money for building costs. The legislature responded with funding to help pay the costs for buildings leased by charter schools. Humphrey Institute students also surveyed students, parents, and graduates of charter public schools and analyzed results as part of masters' programs supervised by CSC staff.

4. Sponsoring the first two statewide polls assessing Minnesotans' attitudes toward charters. February 2003 and 2005 polls conducted by Mason-Dixon Polling, a national company, found strong support among Minnesotans for the charter idea.

5. In the face of many requests for information about how to start charter schools, establishing one of the nation's first charter-school resource centers. This center has hosted conferences, produced publications (two of them offering "best practices" in assessment in small schools and shared facilities, both using examples of outstanding charter and district public schools), and provided information on the center's web site.

Over the past decade, the center has hosted more than twenty statewide or regional meetings inviting both charter and district schools. These conferences have examined themes such as increasing family involvement, increasing student achievement, doing a better job of assessing academic achievement, and using research on service learning/community service.

Charter's Role in Minnesota School Reform
What about the impact of the charter movement on the larger education system? This is not an easy question to answer. But here are a few

changes in Minnesota schools during the last decade that appear to have been influenced, at least in part, by the charter movement:

- In 1989, approximately 4,000 students attended alternative public schools in Minnesota. By 2001, the number had grown to more than 120,000. Alternative schools generally are secondary programs for students who have not succeeded in traditional schools. Growth in the number of alternative schools is not solely a result of the charter movement. But the fact that should districts not respond, the people could create charters, probably influenced districts that started and/or expanded their alternative schools.

- The conversion of small rural elementary schools to charters. In several cases rural school districts decided to listen to families pleading with them not to close a relatively remote elementary school that was a part of a larger district. Instead, local school boards granted charters to community members in Hanska, Echo, Lafayette, and Nerstrand, allowing them to keep these schools open. School boards noted that granting these charters generally was a much more positive, popular action than closing the schools.

- An increase in the number of public-school options serving a cross-section of students. In several communities, proponents of options within the district noted that they preferred creating an option within the district but would create a charter if the district rejected their ideas. In Rochester, the school board agreed to create a school based on E. D. Hirsch's Core Knowledge Curriculum. The Forest Lake board created a Montessori public-school option. In both cases, proponents raised the possibility of creating a charter should the district not accept their proposal.

The dramatic growth of the charter movement suggests that this optimistic view is winning supporters. According to the Center for Education Reform, the number of charters has grown from one serving fewer than a hundred students, to more than 3,400 charters serving more than a million students in 2005. In Minnesota, as in many other states, the charter movement appears to be an illustration of Victor Hugo's dictum: "Stronger than all the armies of the world is an idea whose time has come."

References

Kolderie, Ted
1998   "States Will Have to Withdraw the Exclusive" (rev. ed., available at www.educationevolving.org/pdf/Withdraw_exclusive.pdf

Nathan, Joe
1998   *Charter Schools: Creating Hope and Opportunity in American Education* (rev. ed., paperback). San Francisco: Jossey-Bass.

National Governors' Association/Center for School Change
n.d.   *Providing Quality Options in Education.* Washington, D.C: Authors.

Contributors

John Brandl, compiler, contributor, and editor of this volume, is a professor and former dean of the Humphrey Institute. He has held faculty positions in economics at Boston College, Harvard University, St. John's University (MN), the University of Wisconsin, and the University of the Philippines, and in public administration at the University of Sydney. He has held several positions in federal government, including deputy assistant secretary of the U.S. Department of Health, Education and Welfare, in which he was responsible for the planning, budgeting, and evaluation of the department's efforts in education. Brandl was elected to four terms in the Minnesota House of Representatives and one term in the Minnesota Senate. He has served as president of the Association for Public Policy Analysis and Management. He earned master's and doctoral degrees in economics at Harvard.

John Adams is professor and former director of the Humphrey Institute and professor and former chair of the University of Minnesota's geography department. He researches issues relating to North American cities, urban housing markets and housing policy, and regional economic development in the United States and the former Soviet Union. Adams has also held academic positions at Pennsylvania State University, the University of California at Berkeley, the Economic University of Vienna, Moscow State University, the University of Washington, and the United States Military Academy. He was economic geographer in residence at the Bank of America's world headquarters in San Francisco. He holds a master's degree in economics and a doctorate in geography from the University of Minnesota.

Zbigniew Bochniarz, an economist, is a senior fellow and director of the Humprhey Institute's Center for Nations in Transition. A native of Poland, he has led the institute's efforts in the formerly Communist countries of central and eastern Europe, where he and his colleagues have devised and implemented scores of teaching, research, and advising efforts that support the transition to market democracy. Bochniarz is a founding member of independent, environmental think tanks in Budapest, Prague, Sofia, Warsaw, and Katowice. He is an honorary professor at the University of Warmia and Mazury in Olsztyn, Poland. He holds a doctorate in economics from the Warsaw School of Economics and an honorary doctorate from the University of Miskolc in Hungary.

Harry Boyte, senior fellow, codirects the institute's Center for Democracy and Citizenship. A political philosopher and author of seven books and scores of articles, he also devises and manages practical attempts to engage citizens in public life. He was national coordinator for the New Citizenship, a bipartisan effort to bridge the citizen-government gap. One of the organizations he has formed to help citizens resolve public disputes, Public Achievement, is now operating at many sites in the United States as well as in several other countries. Boyte holds a doctorate in political and social thought from the Union Institute.

John Bryson, professor and associate dean at the Humphrey Institute, works in the areas of leadership, strategic management, and the design of organizational and community change processes. He consults widely in this country and abroad on those subjects, and his book *Strategic Planning for Public and Nonprofit Organizations* is perhaps the best-selling work in the world on that subject. At the institute Bryson led the Reflective Leadership Center, and he founded and directed the Master of Public Affairs program for mid-career students. He holds a doctorate and a master of science degree in urban and regional planning and a master of arts degree in public policy and administration, all from the University of Wisconsin.

Barbara Crosby, associate professor with the Public and Nonprofit Leadership Center at the Humphrey Institute, conducts seminars and workshops in the United States and abroad on leadership and public policy, women in leadership, media and public policy, and organizational leadership. Her book *Leadership for the Common Good,* coauthored with John Bryson, is in its second edition. She was a newspaper reporter and editor and has worked as speechwriter and press secretary for governors in Wisconsin and Minnesota. She has a master's degree in journalism and mass communications from the University of Wisconsin and a doctorate in leadership studies from the Union Institute.

Nancy Eustis, former associate dean of the institute, is professor and director of graduate studies. She is also affiliated with the University of Minnesota's gerontology faculty, sociology department, and School of Public Health. Her research concerns consumer-directed long-term-care services as well as quality and cost-effectiveness of in-home and nursing-home care. During the administration of President Bill Clinton, Eustis was special assistant in disability, aging, and long-term-care policy in the U.S. Department of Health and Human Services. She earned a master of arts degree and a doctorate, both in sociology, at the University of Minnesota.

Thomas Fiutak is a visiting scholar in the University of Minnesota's Department of Educational Policy and Administration. Formerly he was a fellow at the Humphrey Institute and director of its Conflict and Change Center. He conducts research on conflict management and has advised, taught, and facilitated negotiations across the United States and in more than a dozen other countries. He earned a master of science degree in college student personnel services and a doctorate in higher educution and organizational behavior from Indiana University.

Marsha Freeman is a senior lecturer and director of the International Women's Rights Action Watch, a global network (based at the Humphrey Institute) of individuals and groups devoted to monitoring women's rights around the world. An attorney, she was also a reporter for the Minnesota Supreme Court Task Force for Gender Fairness in the Courts. She has a doctorate in English and American literature from the University of Pennsylvania and a law degree from the University of Minnesota.

Morris Kleiner holds the AFL-CIO Chair in Labor Policy and directs the institute's Center for Labor Policy. He is also a faculty member in the University of Minnesota's Industrial Relations Center, and he has been a visiting scholar in the Harvard University Department of Economics and a research fellow at the London School of Economics. Kleiner has been employed with the U.S. Department of Labor and the National Labor Relations Board, and he is a research associate with the National Bureau of Economic Research. He earned a doctorate in economics from the University of Illinois.

Kevin Krizek, assistant professor, teaches courses in land use, transportation, and urban planning. He directs the University of Minnesota's Active Communities/Transportation (ACT) research group, a collection of students and researchers focusing on land-use/transportation policies and programs that influence household residential location decisions and travel behavior. Before coming to the Humphrey Institute, Krizek worked for the American Planning Association, the Teton County (Wyoming) Planning Department, and for a transportation engineering consulting firm. He has a master's degree in planning from the University of North Carolina and a master's of science degree in civil engineering as well as a doctorate in urban design from the University of Washington.

Robert Kudrle, professor, is also an adjunct faculty member with the University of Minnesota Law School. An economist, he studies industrial organization, public policy toward business, and international economic policy. Kudrle has served as a consultant and expert witness for the antitrust division of the U.S. Department of Justice and as a consultant to the Internal Revenue Service. He has been vice president of the International Studies Association. A Rhodes Scholar, he holds a master of philosophy degree in economics from Oxford University and a doctorate in economics from Harvard University.

Ann Markusen, professor, is the director of the Humphrey Institute's Project on Regional and Industrial Economics. She has held faculty positions at Rutgers, Northwestern, the University of California at Berkeley, and the University of Colorado, and she was a Fulbright lecturer in Brazil. She has been an economic policy analyst at the Brookings Institution, a research economist in the Office of the Speaker of the House of Representatives in Michigan, senior fellow at the Council on Foreign Relations, and visiting fellow at the Public Policy Institute of California. Markusen has served as president of the North American Regional Science Association. She holds master of arts and doctoral degrees in economics from Michigan State University.

Lee Munnich, a Humphrey Institute senior fellow and director of the the institute's State and Local Policy Program, focuses on transportation policy, regional economic development, and state and local fiscal policy. He was deputy commissioner of the Minnesota Department of Trade and Economic Development, research director for the Minnesota Business Partnership, economic consultant for the Minnesota House of Representatives, and executive director of the Minnesota Tax Study Commission. Munnich was twice elected to the Minneapolis City Council, and he chaired the National Association of State Development Agencies' research division. He has done postgraduate work in economics and computer science at the University of Minnesota.

Joe Nathan, senior fellow, directs the Humphrey Institute's Center for School Change, which seeks to help transform public education and to produce significant improvements in student achievement. Currently the center is working with governors in six states and with schools in many communities. He has been a public school teacher and administrator and coordinated the National Governors Association education reform project Time for Results. His specialty areas include parent and community involvement, school choice, charter schools, and youth community service. He holds a doctorate in educational administration from the University of Minnesota.

G. Edward Schuh, former dean at the Humphrey Institute, is Regents Professor, the University of Minnesota's highest honor for faculty members. He is also Orville and Jane Freeman Professor in International Trade and Investment Policy and director of the Freeman Center for International Economic Policy at the Humphrey. Upon appointment by the president of the United States, he chaired the Board for International Food and Agricultural Development. A former faculty member and administrator at Purdue University, he has also served as program advisor to the Ford Foundation in Brazil, senior staff economist on the Council of Economic Advisors, deputy undersecretary of the U.S. Department of Agriculture, and as the World Bank's director of agriculture and rural development. He holds a master's degree in agricultural economics from Michigan State University, and master's and doctoral degrees in economics from the University of Chicago. He is professor, honoris causis, at the Federal University of Vicosa and received a doctorate of agriculture, honoris causis, from Purdue University.

The late **Robert Terry** directed the Reflective Leadership Center at the Humphrey Institute. Later he was founder and president of Zobius Leadership International, providing leadership training and mentorship to organizations around the world. He received numerous awards for teaching as well as the Ted Kern Award, the highest honor bestowed on senior executives in the federal government by the Senior Executive Association. He was made an honorary member of government so as to receive the award. Terry received a master in divinity degree from Colgate Rochester Divinity School and master's and doctoral degrees in social ethics from the University of Chicago Divinity School.